Planning for the Wrong Pandemic

Planning for the Wrong Pandemic

Covid-19 and the Limits of Expert Knowledge

ANDREW LAKOFF

polity

First published in 2024 by Polity Press

Polity Press
65 Bridge Street
Cambridge CB2 1UR, UK

Polity Press
111 River Street
Hoboken, NJ 07030, USA

ISBN-13: 978-1-5095-5727-1
ISBN-13: 978-1-5095-5728-8(pb)

A catalogue record for this book is available from the British Library.

Library of Congress Control Number: 2023932670

Typeset in 11 on 14pt Warnock Pro
by Cheshire Typesetting Ltd, Cuddington, Cheshire
Printed and bound in Great Britain by TJ Books Ltd, Padstow, Cornwall

For further information on Polity, visit our website:
politybooks.com

Contents

Preface

During the first weeks and months of the Covid-19 pandemic, in early 2020, I found myself in an unexpected position. Like most everyone else, I was trying to understand what was unfolding in real time, to fathom the harrowing stories reported from places like northern Italy and New York City, to follow scientists' and public health authorities' evolving understanding of the disease, and to manage the complex dynamics of keeping work and family life in motion as the world reeled. At the same time, I was beginning to be called upon as something akin to an "expert" who might be able to provide useful commentary or even counsel to authorities or to the public. This surprising situation was a result of having published, two years before the appearance of the novel coronavirus, a book in the anthropology of science entitled *Unprepared: Global Health in a Time of Emergency*. At the time of its publication, the topic of the book was somewhat obscure to most of my colleagues and friends: how a network of experts in fields like biosecurity and emerging disease had come to worry about and prepare for the onset of a future biological catastrophe. But, in 2020, the book's title led some to credit me – quite mistakenly, I should say – with prescience as the United States appeared, indeed, to have been "unprepared."

But the title of the book had not been meant as a diagnosis or a call to arms. Rather, it alluded to an ethos I had encountered among experts that was accompanied by a distinctive form of rationality. The ethos was one of vigilance toward the possible onset of a deadly new disease, and the rationality involved a systematic approach to envisioning this potential future and mitigating vulnerability to its dangers through techniques such as scenario-based exercises, stockpiling essential supplies, and building systems of surveillance and alert. The book did not take a position as to whether a pandemic was likely to arrive soon; nor did it make a claim about whether health authorities were adequately equipped to manage one if it did. It sought, instead, to characterize an "event in thought" – that is, the invention of a new way of approaching the uncertain and potentially threatening future.

During this period, I was also reaching the final stages of a decade-long collaborative book project, with my co-author Stephen Collier, on the mid-twentieth century history of what we called "emergency government." The focus of our book was a topic that seemed increasingly central to contemporary life but which had been mostly ignored by historians: the invention of a set of governmental practices designed to keep social and economic life in operation in the aftermath of a future catastrophic event.

These two prior projects shaped how I viewed the early stages of the pandemic in the United States – and in particular my sense of how experts and officials were responding to it. Despite the apparent disorder and fragmentation of the country's response, I could not help but notice the centrality of many of the concepts and techniques whose history I had been tracing for the prior decade and a half. This knowledge did not equip me with answers to the pressing questions faced by public health authorities: How can they ensure that essential workers have adequate protective gear. How long should schools and businesses remain shuttered? How soon should experimental treatments be made available? But it did provide me with a distinctive perspective on the debates that were raging about the status of expert knowledge in public life and the legitimate authority of government in managing an emergency. It is that perspective that shapes this book, which asks: How did we come to see this pandemic, this public health emergency, in a particular way? And how did this way of seeing both enable and constrain the actions we took in response?

Acknowledgments

Although this is a short book, I have accumulated numerous debts in its preparation. Many of the ideas in this book have grown out of a long-standing collaboration with Stephen Collier on the history of emergency government in the United States, one that resulted in a much thicker (in both the physical and the ethnographic sense) book than this one. For inspiring intellectual exchanges over the years, well before any of us had heard of the SARS-CoV-2 virus, I'm grateful to Frédéric Keck, Nils Gilman, and Eric Klinenberg. Despite the physical isolation of the pandemic, I never felt intellectually isolated due to the accompaniment of friends and interlocutors. In particular, I want to thank Warwick Anderson, Steve Epstein, Lyle Fearnley, Ben Hurlbut, Chris Kelty, Manjari Mahajan, Janet Roitman, and Kate Zaloom for their timely interventions and encouragements. One of the positive side effects of social distancing for intellectual life was the ability to regularly convene with one's faraway comrades through the wonders of video conferencing. I'm grateful to Talia Dan-Cohen for co-organizing our "expert concepts" group and for energizing conversations with its members: Cameron Brinitzer, Stephen Collier, Hannah Landecker,

Nicolas Langlitz, Rebecca Lemov, and Peter Redfield. And as always, for their nurture (and nature) I thank George Lakoff, Kathleen Frumkin and Robin Lakoff.

I also want to acknowledge some of the venues that were welcoming settings for trying out some of the ideas in this book: the Mellon-Sawyer Seminar on Trust and Mistrust in Experts and Science at Columbia University; the workshop, "After Preparedness," at Sciences-Po in Paris; the "Futures in Question" network hosted by the CRASSH Research Group at the University of Cambridge; the Harvard University Program on Science, Technology, and Society; and the Medical Anthropology Seminar at University College, London. I'm especially grateful to my hosts for these events, including Gil Eyal, Elena Esposito, David Stark, Alexis Bedolla, Sahra Gibbons, Rebecca Irons, David Napier, and Sheila Jasanoff.

Earlier versions of some of the chapters in this book appeared as: "Preparedness Indicators: Measuring the Condition of Global Health Security," in *Sociologica* 15(3) (2021); "The Supply Chain Must Continue," in Thomas J. Sugrue and Caitlin Zaloom (eds), *The Long Year: A 2020 Reader* (Columbia University Press, 2022); "Making Things Fungible," in *Hau* 10(3) (2020); "A Regulatory State of Exception," in Gil Eyal and Thomas Medvetz (eds), *The Oxford Handbook of Expertise and Democratic Politics*; and "The Routes of Viral Traffic," in *Noema* magazine (June 2021).

My editor at Polity, John Thompson, believed in the concept of this book and gently pushed to make it a reality. Christine Wenc's careful editorial eye greatly improved its prose. Thanks also to Helena Heaton and Gail Ferguson for their help throughout the production process.

In the first year of the pandemic (and beyond), as our home became a refuge as well as a place for many new and often challenging kinds of learning, I was exceptionally fortunate to be surrounded by my family's laughter, curiosity, and nourishing support: *un abrazo con tenedor a* Daniela Bleichmar, Natalia Lakoff, and Paloma Lakoff.

During the latter stages of this book's preparation, my uncle Sandy Lakoff died at age 92, having lived, as he put it, "a good and long life." Sandy was a specialist in political thought whose wide-ranging interests included studying the relations between "knowledge and power," which was the title of a collection he edited in 1966. I wish he could have read this book, though I am certain he would have had some suggestions for its improvement.

Abbreviations

ASPR:	Assistant Secretary of Preparedness and Response
BARDA:	Biomedical Advanced Research and Development Authority
BLA:	Biologics License Application
CDC:	Centers for Disease Control
CISA:	Cybersecurity and Infrastructure Security Agency
DHS:	Department of Homeland Security
EUA:	Emergency Use Authorization
FDA:	Food and Drug Administration
FEMA:	Federal Emergency Management Agency
GHSA:	Global Health Security Agenda
GHSI:	Global Health Security Index
HHS:	Department of Health and Human Services
IHR:	International Health Regulations
NIH:	National Institutes of Health
NSC:	National Security Council
NSRB:	National Security Resources Board
ODM:	Office of Defense Mobilization
PHEIC:	public health emergency of international concern
SNS:	Strategic National Stockpile
WHO:	World Health Organization

Introduction

"We're very, very ready for this." It was late February 2020, and President Trump was introducing the White House Coronavirus Task Force to an assembled group of reporters. Only fifteen cases of Covid-19 had so far been reported in the United States, and the president expressed confidence that his administration's policies would keep the disease from spreading widely.[1] Over the next year, this optimism would prove tragically ill-founded as the estimated number of deaths caused by the disease climbed to a half-million and beyond. Indeed, the country's belated, disorganized, and fractured response to the coronavirus pandemic would prompt many observers to ask why the United States had been caught so apparently unprepared. Critics pointed to a series of candidates for blame: a president who was dismissive of scientific expertise and indifferent to the task of leading the government's response; a slow-footed bureaucracy incapable of flexible response to a rapidly changing situation; a decentralized public health system that had long been starved of resources; a fragmented media landscape that enabled rumors and misinformation to prosper; preexisting social disparities that heightened inequities in the impact of the disease; and more.[2]

But, at least in this case, there was a certain basis to the president's bombast: US officials and experts had been anticipating and planning for a catastrophic infectious disease outbreak for more than two decades. In the late 1990s, the Department of Health and Human Services established a national stockpile of medical supplies to be used in a future public health emergency. In 2005, the White House released a national strategy for addressing the threat of a future pandemic, outlining the roles to be played by federal, state and local governments, the private sector, and individual citizens. Meanwhile, think tanks and federal agencies held a series of scenario-based exercises, from Dark Winter in 2001 to Crimson Contagion in 2019, designed to test the government's ability to manage a catastrophic disease outbreak. Over this period, Congress enacted numerous laws and amendments to provide the executive branch with the administrative mechanisms and discretionary resources needed to address a nationwide public health emergency. And the National Institutes of Health provided millions of dollars in grant support for basic research in virology to enable the detection and rapid containment of emerging pathogens. Having invested in these and other preparations, the United States was widely considered to be the world's leader in pandemic preparedness.

Not only had the federal government been anticipating such an event over the prior two decades; many of its preparedness plans were rapidly implemented in the first months of the Covid-19 pandemic. Let us take, for example, the concept of "flattening the curve," which seemed to appear out of nowhere in March 2020. In fact, it dated from 2007 guidelines issued by the Centers for Disease Control for the community management of a potential avian influenza pandemic. The concept was accompanied by an image of two possible epidemic trajectories, one steeper and shorter in duration than the other. It was an image of two potential futures. In the future in which we did not take the necessary actions, a sudden influx of Covid-19 cases would overwhelm the healthcare system: medical personnel would fall sick, essential supplies would run short, and intensive care units would overflow with desperately ill patients. In the future represented by the other, flatter curve, our interventions would slow down the rate of disease transmission and extend the total number of cases over a longer period, allowing the health system to make the necessary adjustments. To flatten the curve was a collective injunction, pointing to a series of actions that public health authorities as well as normal citizens could take to address the pandemic emergency: shift schools to remote learning, work from home, cancel gatherings, and close public spaces. The image of an epidemic curve whose contours would be shaped by our present actions helped make the otherwise invisible specter of a rapidly spreading virus into something that could be understood and worked on.[3]

At the same time, however, authorities' efforts to flatten the curve had certain unanticipated side effects that only became apparent as the pandemic wore on. For one, the social distancing measures designed to slow the rate of disease transmission had starkly unequal consequences. Some employees were able to smoothly shift to working from home whereas others lost their jobs as stores and restaurants were shuttered; meanwhile, those workers classified as "essential" were in many cases required to labor on site without adequate protection from the risk of infection. Similarly, students' ability to adapt to remote learning differed in relation to the wealth of their households and the means of their school districts. Moreover, it was not clear how long the set of policies enacted to flatten the curve would have to be implemented. As the period of social distancing extended, political struggles began to erupt over issues such as the authority of the state to govern individual behavior, the validity of public health expertise, and how to balance the benefits of reducing disease incidence against the costs of school and business closures. Many state and local governments became hesitant about, or even hostile to, the prospect of imposing restrictive measures over an unspecified time horizon.

To understand why the side effects of health authorities' efforts to flatten the curve had not been foreseen, we must look at the context in which the concept was initially developed. In the mid-2000s, roughly a decade and a half before the onset of Covid-19, public health authorities were gravely worried about the potential onset of an H5N1 avian influenza pandemic. Such a prospect raised the question of how to contain a rapidly spreading and highly pathogenic strain of influenza in the absence of effective biomedical interventions. A group of historians proposed a novel approach to the problem, drawing on archival research that compared different cities' responses to the 1918 flu pandemic – the last time the population had been faced with a virulent strain of flu to which there was little immunity.[4] The research demonstrated that cities that had proactively cancelled public gatherings and closed schools in anticipation of an epidemic wave had fared better than cities that had been slow to enact such measures. Based on these findings, the historians suggested the incorporation of "nonpharmaceutical interventions" – what would come to be known as social distancing measures – into the government's pandemic preparedness plans. The Centers for Disease Control adopted this approach in its 2007 "pre-pandemic planning guidance," which laid out nonpharmaceutical interventions to be taken in relation to different phases of an envisioned influenza pandemic.[5] Thus in early 2020, the concept was already at hand, rapidly applied by public health officials to slow the spread of the novel coronavirus through the population. But the measure had been envisioned in relation to a different virus, one with different characteristics. As one of the historians who helped devise the mitigation strategy later recalled, his team had not "imagined a stubborn, persistent pathogen like the novel coronavirus." Rather, "we were thinking of influenza."[6] With influenza in mind, they had assumed that social distancing measures would be necessary for just a few months before a vaccine became available or the epidemic wave receded as temperatures rose in the spring. And given its narrow focus on mitigating the spread of disease, the policy did not foresee the political conflicts that its prescribed measures might spark.

The nonpharmaceutical interventions associated with flattening the curve were just one element within a broader framework of preparedness that guided the government's early response to the novel coronavirus. As authorities sought to address an urgent and uncertain situation, they relied on a set of available concepts and tools – organizational schemes, mitigation guidelines, modes of classification, regulatory protocols – that had been devised for managing a future pandemic emergency. This heterogeneous set of governmental devices enabled officials to take hold of the event, to make sense of it, and to rapidly implement policies in response. In this sense, the pandemic should not be seen as an external visitation that unfolded independently of our ways of understanding and managing it; rather, it was in relation to such devices that it was constituted as a comprehensible event. At the same time, however, the actual coronavirus pandemic, as it unfolded, defied many of the assumptions that were embedded in these devices.

The framework of preparedness had been assembled by an array of experts and authorities over the course of several decades in anticipation of a range of potential catastrophes, from nuclear war to major natural disasters to a bioterrorist attack. Two prior periods are especially significant in this regard. The first is the early Cold War, when mobilization planners sought to prepare for the potential occurrence of a catastrophic future event – a nuclear attack on the United States. The problem they sought to address was how to ensure the continued operation of the nation's critical systems – such as energy, transportation, and food provision – in the aftermath of such an attack. They developed a schema of emergency government that included tools for mitigating urban vulnerability, plans for allocating scare resources in a crippled economy, and a blueprint for the reorganization of government to address the pressing demands of a wartime emergency. With such plans in place, the shift to emergency mode in the wake of a nuclear attack would not require the declaration of a state of exception but would be situated within the existing constitutional-legal order. Over the course of the 1950s, planners tested and revised this schema through a program of scenario-based exercises that simulated the effects of a future attack, exposing gaps in preparedness that could then be addressed in revised plans.[7]

The second key period begins roughly four decades later, when these existing techniques for governing a future emergency were redeployed to address the newly perceived threat of a catastrophic disease outbreak. In the late 1990s, US national security officials became increasingly worried about the prospect of a bioweapons attack, leading to the establishment of a national stockpile of biomedical countermeasures. Then, in the aftermath of 9/11 and the anthrax letters that followed, security officials pursued further biodefense-related initiatives such as Project BioShield (2004), which enabled the federal government to procure novel countermeasures against pathogenic threats such as smallpox and anthrax through contracting arrangements with biotech and pharmaceutical companies. Meanwhile, after the 2003 SARS outbreak, and as the specter of an avian influenza pandemic loomed, biological preparedness was extended to address naturally occurring infectious diseases. Among other measures, federal agencies developed pandemic preparedness plans, antiviral medications were added to the national stockpile, and federal research agencies sought to incentivize innovation in vaccine development.

These efforts expanded internationally as US health officials pushed for investment in the new field of "global health security." With support from the Centers for Disease Control, the World Health Organization (WHO) adopted a set of new regulations focusing on the detection and containment of emerging infectious diseases.[8] The release of its 2007 report, *A Safer Future: Global Public Health Security in the 21st Century*, marked a coordinated effort to implement the techniques of public health preparedness at a global scale.[9] Events such as the 2009 H1N1 influenza pandemic and the 2014 Ebola epidemic in West Africa resulted in further US-led initiatives such as the Global Health Security Agenda, which sought to implement core capacities for managing outbreaks of emerging diseases in resource-poor settings. As the nation that had initiated and provided support for many of these efforts, the United States was a driving force in the global extension of pandemic preparedness.[10]

It is not so much that the United States found itself unprepared for a pandemic in the spring of 2020, but rather that officials and planners had been anticipating something different. From the early stages of the coronavirus pandemic, a set of governmental devices that had been developed in relation to prior contexts was applied to a novel disease. The availability of these devices made it possible to act on an unfolding situation even as its contours were not yet known, but it also led to blind spots and unanticipated outcomes, in many cases due to assumptions that were built into the framework of preparedness. This book asks: under what circumstances were the key elements of this framework invented – what problems were they initially designed to solve? What did these concepts and tools enable experts and officials to see, and what did they hide from view? How did they shape the controversies that arose around the role of experts and government in the public health response? And, finally, as we assess the failures of our response to the pandemic and begin to prepare for "the next one," to what extent should we take for granted the capacity of these tools to effectively guide our future interventions?

Expertise in crisis

Planning for the Wrong Pandemic focuses mostly on the first year of the coronavirus pandemic, when many of the key controversies around the governmental response in the United States initially arose. The book takes a genealogical approach to the analysis of these controversies, looking at the settings in which now taken-for-granted concepts and tools were invented. The goal of such an approach is not to weigh in on one side or the other of fractious public debates, whether over the efficacy of a certain policy or the legitimacy of a certain mandate. Rather, it asks about the assumptions that are tacitly embedded within a given technical solution: what was the problem to which this solution was initially addressed, and how did this prior context shape our later response to a different situation? As the philosopher Ian Hacking writes, this approach investigates "how our present concepts were made," and, crucially, "how the conditions for their formation constrain our current ways of thinking."[11]

Each chapter of the book focuses on an expert concept or technique that was key to the pandemic response in the United States: the preparedness indicator, essential workers, the Strategic National Stockpile, the scenario-based exercise, the Emergency Use Authorization, and gain-of-function research. Until early 2020, most of these concepts and techniques were little known to the public, tucked away in regulatory protocols, interagency committees or think tank reports, and under the aegis of obscure government agencies like the office of the Assistant Secretary for Preparedness within the Department of Health and Human Services or the Cybersecurity and Infrastructure Agency within the Department of Homeland Security. The chapters thus focus on forms of expert knowledge that come into play in managing a public health emergency. They do not, for the most part, emphasize the production of biomedical knowledge in areas like virology or immunology; rather, they look at forms of knowledge that consider infectious disease as a governmental problem: the logistics of vaccine distribution, methods for evaluating the risk of experimental treatments, or expertise in scenario development. Many of the contests over authoritative knowledge that occurred during the pandemic had more to do with such forms of technocratic expertise than with biomedical knowledge about the disease itself.[12] Take, for example, the question of how to fairly distribute scarce medical supplies, or the debate over thresholds for public health agency decisions about opening schools and businesses. In this sense, such controversies are misunderstood insofar as they are seen as a question of public trust in science per se. At stake was not so much whether one "believed in science" in general as how much, in an uncertain and politically charged situation, one trusted in the legitimacy of technocratic authority or the validity of expert claims. What made the tension around expert knowledge claims especially fraught was the peculiar circumstance that, at the outset of the most significant public health crisis in a century, a populist movement avowedly opposed to technocratic authority occupied the very executive branch that was charged with leading a necessarily expert-driven response.

While the focus of the book is on the US response, the application of the expert concepts and techniques described in this book was not limited to a single national context. In the years before the pandemic, scenario-based exercises had been conducted by numerous national governments and multilateral organizations; other countries had built medical stockpiles and had made preparedness plans. While many of the governmental devices that are central to pandemic preparedness – from the classification of essential workers to the global health security indicator – were initially developed in the United States, they have since been adopted in a range of other settings. What was perhaps distinctive to the US case was the striking disjuncture between public expectations of governmental capacity, on the one hand, and the actual response, on the other.

The first chapter addresses this disjuncture by looking at a measuring device for comparing levels of national preparedness, the "global health security indicator." In October 2019, two think tanks based in Washington, DC released a comparative study that ranked the United States first among 195 countries in its "readiness to deal with the threat of an epidemic or pandemic."[13] Despite this impressive ranking, one year later the US mortality rate from Covid-19 was significantly higher than that of lower-ranked countries such as Germany, South Korea, and Vietnam. The chapter investigates this apparent puzzle by asking what task the global health security indicator was invented to accomplish. This concept was introduced in 2016 as part of a long-standing effort among global health authorities to incentivize poor countries to implement the technical capacities seen at the time to be critical for outbreak detection and response. As it turned out, the technical capacities measured by the global health security indicators had little to do with each country's success in responding to the coronavirus pandemic. Nonetheless, the question of what *was* measured by such indicators provides insight into the limits of global health security as it was construed by experts in advance of the pandemic. The project of global health security, it seems, was better equipped to contain an Ebola outbreak than to manage the social, economic, and political ramifications of Covid-19.

Chapter 2 looks at the category of "essential workers," which was introduced in tandem with government authorities' early efforts to flatten the curve of disease incidence. The category was used to identify groups whose continued work on site was necessary to keep vital systems, such as transportation and food production, operational while much of social and economic life was shut down. It soon became an object of political contention as those workers deemed essential often did not have the privilege of avoiding the risk of infection. At the same time, various industries, from cannabis sellers to gun manufacturers, sought reclassification as "essential" in order to avoid the shutdown of their operations. Less well understood in these discussions was the background to this technique of classification. It had been introduced two decades earlier as part of a federal program to ensure the continued operation of critical infrastructures in the aftermath of a catastrophic event such as a mass-casualty terrorist attack. But its genealogy can be traced back further to a mid-twentieth-century conceptualization of collective life as composed of vulnerable, vital systems – an understanding that initially arose in the context of interwar air targeting and then was transposed to Cold War mobilization planning. More than a half-century later, a category originally devised to reduce vulnerability at the level of the system generated a novel form of risk at the level of the individual – the risk of being classified as essential.

Chapter 3 investigates the history of a future-oriented technique, medical stockpiling. In the early stages of the pandemic, the public learned about a vast storehouse of essential supplies known as the "Strategic National Stockpile," managed by the US federal government for use in a future health emergency. Unfortunately, it turned out that the stockpile did not contain nearly enough essential medical supplies, such as masks, gowns and ventilators, to address surging demand, leading to desperate competition among states and localities for a dwindling stock of these items. The stockpile did, however, contain warehouses full of medical supplies that were not needed during the pandemic, such as large quantities of smallpox vaccine, anthrax medication, and nerve-gas antidote. This chapter addresses the question of why the stockpile, envisioned for a certain kind of future emergency, was ill-equipped for the emergency that actually occurred. The chapter considers the history of medical stockpiling as a governmental technique, focusing on two periods: first, the Cold War-era establishment of a civil defense stockpile of medical supplies for use after a nuclear attack; and second, the creation of a National Pharmaceutical Stockpile in the late 1990s, in the context of anxiety among national security officials about the prospect of a bioweapons attack. This historical trajectory points to the temporal paradox of the stockpile: it is put together with a particular future in view, but its contents remain frozen in the moment of its assembly.

Chapter 4 examines another technique that seeks to envision a possible future, the scenario-based exercise. As glaring problems in the US response became apparent in the first months of the pandemic, critical observers noted that many of these problems had been anticipated in test exercises conducted by the federal government in recent years. If officials had been made aware of such problems by these exercises, why were they not addressed? To answer this question, the chapter investigates what scenario-based exercises are actually meant to accomplish. It traces the invention of the scenario-based exercise to the mid-1950s, when it was introduced to test plans to ensure the continuity of government in the wake of a nuclear attack. The chapter then turns to the example of "Crimson Contagion," a pandemic simulation organized by the federal government in 2019. Like the preparedness exercises of the Cold War, this exercise had a narrow purview: it was not designed to open novel areas to scrutiny but rather to galvanize attention to already identified targets of administrative reform.

A characteristic feature of emergency government, as it was developed in the mid-twentieth-century United States, is the use of administrative devices to enable flexible response to an unprecedented situation requiring urgent intervention. Chapter 5 focuses on one such device, the Emergency Use Authorization (EUA), designed to accelerate the regulatory authorization of experimental medical treatments upon the declaration of a public health emergency. The EUA procedure was introduced as part of the Project BioShield Act of 2004, with the scenario in mind of a bioterrorist attack that would require the rapid distribution to the public of an as yet unapproved medication.

A decade and a half later, the procedure was critical to the accelerated development and distribution of a vaccine against Covid-19. However, its application during the coronavirus pandemic had an unanticipated side effect: the very flexibility that enabled the rapid authorization of an experimental vaccine also threatened to undermine public confidence in the regulatory process. Meant as a technical fix to an envisioned regulatory bottleneck, its designers did not foresee the potential for its abuse by an opportunistic executive branch in the context of a bitterly fought presidential election campaign.

The final chapter of the book looks at the development of a preparedness technique whose purpose is to anticipate a potential pandemic but which may also hold the danger of starting one: gain-of-function research. To elucidate the assumptions underlying this technique, the chapter tells the story of the global extension of pandemic preparedness in the decades before the appearance of Covid-19. Beginning in the late 1980s, a group of infectious-disease specialists claimed that the emergence of novel infectious diseases such as Ebola and AIDS was the result of processes of late modernity: environmental degradation, rural-to-urban migration, and intensifying global circulation. The only way to address the ongoing threat posed by emerging pathogens, they argued, would be to monitor their onset and contain them before they spread widely. This goal of pandemic prevention set in motion a program, funded by the US federal government, which involved gathering viral samples from wildlife populations and manipulating them in laboratories to test their potential to start a pandemic. Here scientists used methods of genetic manipulation to determine what changes in the virus might lead to increased transmissibility among mammals. In the spring of 2021, this kind of research became a site of public controversy as critics, pointing to work taking place at the Wuhan Institute of Virology, suggested that, rather than prevent a pandemic, such research might instead have sparked one. However, the question of the pandemic's origin remained open into 2024, more than four years after its onset, and it was unclear when, if ever, it would be settled. The chapter closes with a reflection on this condition of diagnostic uncertainty, pointing to the difficulty of proceeding with post hoc assessment and critical rectification in anticipation of "the next one" in the absence of a definitive judgment as to what caused this one.

The protagonists in this book are concepts and devices that are brought to bear in an emergency and that, unbeknownst to their users, may carry with them tacit assumptions that structure what kinds of questions can be asked and what responses are possible. Some readers may wonder where the people are in this story. The book's suggestion is that these devices fundamentally shaped how we understood and responded to the pandemic. When we stayed at home to flatten the curve, when we took a new Covid vaccine or hesitated about doing so, or when we wondered whether we should still be wearing N95 masks in public places, our experience of the pandemic was mediated by the expert concepts and devices that gave the event a certain form and coherence. And yet we were much more likely to be aware of the concepts themselves than of the tacit assumptions that were borne within them. In this sense, the knowledge forms described in the book are not located diffusely in a cultural imagination or in a collective consciousness. In fact, their ambit may be rather circumscribed, situated in the decision tools wielded by often unknown government bureaucrats or think tank intellectuals. But insofar as they guide the work of experts and authorities in governing an emergency, we may well find ourselves under their influence. To analyze the limits of these concepts and devices should not be mistaken as an attack on technocracy or on the authority of expert knowledge. Rather, it is an argument for experts – and the rest of us – to be aware of the assumptions that underlie the tools we have inherited and that shape our decisions in the face of an urgent and uncertain situation.

1

Preparedness Indicators

In October 2019, two Washington, DC-based think tanks, the Nuclear Threat Initiative and the Center for Health Security, released a report entitled the Global Health Security Index (GHSI). According to its Executive Summary, the GHSI was "the first comprehensive assessment and benchmarking of health security and related capabilities" among the state parties to the revised International Health Regulations.[1] Led by biosecurity expert Elizabeth Cameron of the Nuclear Threat Initiative and epidemiologist Jennifer Nuzzo of the Center for Health Security, the index project was funded by philanthropic organizations such as the Bill and Melinda Gates Foundation and supported by an international panel of experts drawn from multilateral organizations, national health ministries, and universities.

When the SARS-CoV-2 virus began to spread globally in early 2020, the GHSI rankings initially provided the White House with a source of reassurance. In introducing the Coronavirus Task Force to the press, President Trump held aloft a copy of the report. After comparing the "countries best and worst prepared for an epidemic," he boasted, the experts who conducted the study had concluded that "the United States, we're rated number one." And indeed, the experts' report had ranked the United States first among all WHO member states in its "readiness to deal with the threat of an epidemic or pandemic." This finding was perhaps unsurprising, given the country's significant investment in public health preparedness during the prior two decades. But over the course of the following year, as the nation's failure to adequately respond to the Covid-19 pandemic became clear, the index's rankings provoked widespread puzzlement.[2] The United States had been ranked well ahead of countries that, in terms of per capita fatality rates, proved far more successful in managing Covid-19 during the first year of the pandemic, including South Korea (ranked #9 on the Index), Germany (#14), Singapore (#24) and Vietnam (#50). While the Index "purports to predict the potential performance of countries during the outbreak of a pandemic," a group of science policy scholars summarized, "the actual performances during Covid-19 were largely the opposite of these predictions."[3] How was it possible, as an editorial in the *Washington Post* put it in late 2020, that the United States, which had been "ranked best in the world" the previous year among 195 countries in "how well prepared they were for an outbreak of infectious disease," could now find itself "among the hardest-hit nations in the world?" Insofar as the United States "was supposed to be equipped to handle a pandemic," the editorial asked, "What went wrong?"[4]

Commentators offered a range of explanations for the discrepancy between the GHSI's 2019 rankings of countries' readiness and their actual performances in responding to the pandemic. For *New York Times* columnist Nicholas Kristof, the contrast was evidence of a "colossal failure of leadership" by the Trump administration: "the paradox is that a year ago, the United States seemed particularly well positioned to handle this kind of crisis."[5] Other critical observers speculated that the explanation for the discrepancy must have to do with the way the GHSI had measured pandemic preparedness.

As economist Branko Milanovic wrote, "[A]n index whose objective was to highlight strengths and weaknesses in the handling of potential pandemics has either entirely failed, or can be shown to have been useless." Political analyst Ezra Klein explained that the index had failed because it was "measuring the wrong things." Rather than emphasizing technical capabilities like reference laboratories or vaccine-production capacity, Klein argued, it should have focused on what proved to be more consequential factors in a successful response, such as levels of "trust in government and trust in fellow citizens."[6] Or perhaps the very attempt to quantitatively assess the national characteristics critical for successful pandemic response was misguided. While "political will is needed to protect people from the consequences of epidemics," as science and policy scholar Sheila Jasanoff put it, "one may ask how a model of national capabilities built mainly on measurable indicators of health security was intended to account for such an intangible and volatile concept."[7] For still others, the disjuncture between the index's health security rankings and actual pandemic outcomes undermined the very premise of governmental investment in preparedness measures. As two economists concluded, "regardless of how we cut the data or adjust for other factors, a similar story emerges – pandemic preparedness had very little influence on the course of the pandemic."[8]

More generally, the GHSI rankings served as a lens through which commentators could project their own understandings of what had led to success or failure in national responses to Covid-19. Thus, journalist Michael Lewis opened his book, *The Premonition*, with a comparison between public health and the world of sport, describing the index as "what amounted to a preseason college football ranking for one hundred ninety-five countries."[9] According to this analogy, "the United States was the [Texas] Longhorns of pandemic preparedness" – wealthy, with access to talent as well as "special relationships with the experts whose votes determined the rankings." But then "the game was played" and "preseason rankings no longer mattered." In the book's narrative of the US government's sclerotic response, three maverick public health experts wrestle with a bureaucratic apparatus that is crippled by institutional malaise and chronic risk aversion. Similarly, the Covid Crisis Group, a set of experts assembled in 2020 by four philanthropies to proactively assess the US pandemic response, framed its investigative report, *Lessons from the Covid War*, with a reference to the GHSI, calling it "a landmark index of health security capabilities." Although "some people later mocked this index" for ranking the United States highest in the world, "the authors worked hard to measure what they could." But appearances could be deceiving, the report pointed out, foreshadowing its overall diagnosis of the sources of the US failure: "it is hard to measure competence" and it is difficult "to size up the human and institutional software that translates assets into effective performance."[10]

Although they differed in their interpretation of the significance of the mismatch between the GHSI's ratings and actual outcomes, these various analyses all shared the assumption that the index had been intended as a predictive tool – that it promised to gauge future levels of national success in responding to a pandemic. Judged on this basis, the US response to Covid-19 clearly belied its high ranking. But in fact the index was intended for a different purpose. It was designed not as a device for anticipating the future but rather as a tool for global governance in the present. By looking at what it sought to govern, and how, we can better understand why the GHSI measured some things and not others – and why its rankings did not anticipate later markers of success in managing the pandemic. As we will see, the index embodied a particular vision of the future of infectious disease – one that was grounded in the experience of the recent past. Let us begin, then, with a different question than the one posed by the observers mentioned above: not why the index failed to correctly predict outcomes but, rather, what was the problem to which the creation of a tool for measuring a given country's condition of "health security" was meant as a possible solution? Here we need to turn back to the moment, roughly three decades before the appearance of SARS-CoV-2, when the field of global health security was first established, along with its central object of concern, "emerging infectious disease."

Constituting global health security

One of the earliest articulations of the rationale underlying global health security can be found in a 1988 speech by Nobel prizewinning microbial geneticist Joshua Lederberg. The speech, later reprinted in the *Journal of the American Medical Association*, was entitled "Medical Science, Infectious Disease, and the Unity of Humankind." Speaking at the height of the AIDS pandemic, Lederberg urged his audience to consider AIDS as a harbinger for the future. "We will face similar catastrophes again, and will be ever more confounded in dealing with them, if we do not come to grips with the realities of the place of our species in nature." The place of humans in nature was one pervaded with viral exchanges, according to Lederberg, and therefore the ongoing emergence of novel pathogens was an inexorable process. In his speech, Lederberg argued for the need to invest in research on viral emergence in other parts of the world, on the basis not of humanitarian concern for others but rather that of self-protection against encroaching threats: "No matter how selfish our motives, we can no longer be indifferent to the suffering of others," he pronounced. "The microbe that felled one child in a distant continent can reach yours today and seed a global pandemic tomorrow."[11] Lederberg was part of a loose network of infectious-disease specialists who sought to raise awareness of the danger posed by what they termed "emerging infections," and to stimulate research in the increasingly neglected field of tropical medicine. The group also included epidemiologist D. A. Henderson, who had led the WHO campaign to eradicate smallpox in the 1970s, as well as the eminent virologist Robert Shope. Lederberg and Shope were co-editors of an influential 1992 Institute of Medicine report, *Emerging Infections: Microbial Threats to Health in the United States,* which pointed to "the critical importance of vigilance for infectious disease" in the wake of the "emergence of HIV disease and AIDS, the reemergence of tuberculosis, and the increased opportunity for disease spread through international travel."[12]

Over the next several years, bestselling journalistic accounts such as *The Coming Plague* by Laurie Garrett and *The Hot Zone* by Richard Preston popularized these scientists' argument that, despite years of medical progress, the advanced industrial world was increasingly vulnerable to the onset of deadly new pathogens.[13] According to this vision, emerging infections had three salient characteristics. First, novelty: their appearance in human populations and potential for rapid spread were bound up with phenomena of late modernity – increased urban density, environmental degradation, and global interdependence were the ecological conditions of possibility for infectious disease emergence.[14] Second, vulnerability: while these diseases typically emerged in poorer parts of the world, intensifying circulation rendered citizens of wealthy countries vulnerable to them. And third, inevitability: the ongoing emergence of potentially devastating infectious diseases such as AIDS and Ebola could not be prevented but could only be monitored – and, ideally, managed before they spread widely to become catastrophic – through the establishment of a network of detection and containment. It would be necessary to construct a global system for "regulating viral traffic," as epidemiologist Stephen Morse put it, in order to address this novel threat.[15]

In the wake of failures in the mid-1990s by national health ministries in poor countries to report and adequately respond to outbreaks of Ebola and plague, international health officials sought a means to improve the world's ability to manage outbreaks of emerging (and reemerging) infectious diseases. They proposed to revise the venerable International Health Regulations (IHR) as a mechanism to foster collaboration across national borders. A descendant of late nineteenth-century conventions to control the spread of diseases such as cholera and yellow fever, the IHR are a legally binding agreement among WHO member states designed to ensure national sovereignty over public health response to an infectious disease outbreak while at the same time regulating state action to minimize global economic disruption and ensure that international authorities can monitor and minimize the spread of the disease.[16] The IHR system envisions the WHO role as one of organizational coordination and technical support rather than operational response, a role that assumes the capacity for effective public health interventions at the national level. Thus, the IHR provides administrative and technical protocols for managing the global circulation of pathogens as a collaboration between multilateral organizations and national authorities.

The 2003 SARS outbreak provided further impetus for revision of the International Health Regulations. Following the vision that had been articulated by Lederberg and his colleagues a decade and a half earlier, international health authorities conceptualized SARS in terms of the novel threat posed by emerging infections: global populations had been rendered vulnerable to such an outbreak due to new forms of human–animal interaction, rapid international travel, and the absence of a global network for detection and response to novel pathogens. From this perspective, the Chinese government's initial response to SARS pointed to a more general problem: national governments were often either incapable of detecting or unwilling to report outbreaks of novel infectious disease to international health officials, or to allow experts into the country to monitor and manage such outbreaks. According to international health authorities, this problem at the national level posed a grave danger to the world's health security. Epidemiologist David Heymann, a veteran of the US Centers for Disease Control's Epidemiological Intelligence Service who moved to the WHO to work on its AIDS program, articulated this concern in a 2004 interview: "inadequate surveillance and response capacity in a single country can endanger the public health security of national populations and in the rest of the world."[17] Thus, efforts to reform the IHR system focused on improving national capacities for surveillance and response, particularly in countries in the developing world that were seen as likely sites of disease emergence.

The revised IHR, enacted by WHO member states in 2005 after a decade of planning and negotiation, included three major changes to address the threat posed by emerging infections. First, it expanded the set of diseases whose detection required the notification of international authorities beyond the existing list of yellow fever, cholera, and plague, introducing the generic category of "public health emergency of international concern" (PHEIC) since the pathogen to be detected might not yet be known. Here the regulations defined the actions the WHO would take in order to coordinate a global response to the declaration of a PHEIC as well as the responsibilities of national partner organizations. Second, in order to deal with national health ministries' reluctance to report outbreaks, the revised IHR allowed for the WHO to officially recognize reports coming from non-national reporting systems such as the Global Outbreak Alert and Response Network. And finally, in order to establish the collaborative network seen as necessary for managing future outbreaks, it obliged all WHO member states to develop a set of "core capacities for surveillance and response." It was this latter revision that would eventually lead to the development of the Global Health Security Index. The core capacities required by the revised IHR included outbreak detection and alert, the determination of control measures, and the establishment of a national public health emergency plan.[18]

A 2007 WHO report, *A Safer Future: Global Public Health Security in the 21st Century*, spelled out the agenda of the revised IHR – to ensure the ability to contain emerging infections at a global scale. The report emphasized the need for collaboration between national and international authorities: global health security could be achieved only "if there is immediate alert and response to disease outbreaks and other incidents that could spark epidemics or spread globally and if there are national systems in place for detection and response should such events occur across international borders."[19] However, the project of establishing such a system of global health security faced a significant practical challenge: national governments would not only have to collaborate with international health authorities but would also have to build the technical capacities to enable such collaboration. According to the revised IHR, each state party was required to fulfill the "core capacities" requirement by 2012. But the agreement included neither a legal mechanism of enforcement nor an allotment of resources that would support the implementation of these capacities across all 193 WHO member states.

By the 2012 deadline, only 20 percent of WHO member states had fulfilled the IHR core capacities requirement, and WHO extended its deadline for compliance to 2016.[20] Two years later, a new organizational actor entered the picture, the Global Health Security Agenda (GHSA). The goal of the GHSA was to stimulate investment in building core capacities in poor countries. As health security analysts Jennifer Nuzzo and Matthew Shearer wrote, the program sought to "jump-start stalled progress toward implementation of the IHR by increasing national support for IHR implementation."[21] While the GHSA was cast as a multi-country initiative, the funding and organizational impetus for the program came from the United States. The program was launched in early 2014 by the

US Centers for Disease Control (CDC), with a US$40 million pledge geared to help countries around the world "establish minimum capabilities" as outlined in the revised IHR. Echoing the argument that had been made by Joshua Lederberg two and a half decades earlier, CDC director Tom Frieden pointed to security rather than altruism as the rationale for US taxpayer investment in health infrastructure in other parts of the world. "US national security depends on global health security," he explained in introducing the program, "because a threat anywhere is a threat everywhere."[22] The GHSA laid out a collaborative process through which a given country's "capability for health security" would be strengthened via donors' contributions: if the country participated in a joint process of assessment led by technical experts and developed a plan for improving its core capacities, it would be eligible for funding and training support from GHSA partners, principally the US Centers for Disease Control.

After Ebola

The 2014 Ebola epidemic in West Africa led US health authorities to push more aggressively for the implementation of the IHR's core capacity requirement. In the aftermath of what was widely seen as a catastrophic failure of global health response, post hoc assessments blamed the international community – and the WHO in particular – for allowing what a UN report called a "preventable tragedy" to unfold.[23] Over ten thousand people had died from a disease that in prior outbreaks had never caused more than a few hundred deaths. In their assessments of the global response to the epidemic, international health authorities interpreted the event as a failed test of the IHR system – one that should lead to a process of diagnosis and self-rectification. As an internal WHO report on the agency's Ebola response put it, the epidemic had been a "major test of the revised IHR": the "severity and duration" of the epidemic had "challenged the IHR in unprecedented ways," shining "a bright light on just how ill-prepared and vulnerable the global community remains."[24]

In their assessments of the global response to Ebola, experts focused on flaws in the implementation of the revised IHR framework. In particular, the WHO's failure to enforce compliance with the IHR's core capacities requirement was implicated in the poor response by national public health agencies in the region affected by the epidemic. Despite the IHR's aspiration of "strengthening health systems everywhere" as "the best defence against outbreaks of potential international concern," an editorial in *Nature* argued, "the reality is that few poor countries have anything that resembles a working outbreak-response system."[25] In explaining the failure to build a functioning system of global health security, the WHO post hoc report blamed "weak political will and limited awareness and understanding of the IHR and its requirements at the highest levels of national governments," as well as "inadequate financial resources and expertise to establish the core capacities" for making it impossible for most countries to implement IHR requirements.[26]

From the perspective of US health authorities, the Ebola epidemic confirmed Frieden's warning of the country's vulnerability to emerging disease threats coming from other parts of the world. In the fall of 2014, as the epidemic threatened to spread globally and the first cases appeared in the United States, Congress had allocated US$3.7 billion in emergency funds to the United States Agency for International Development (USAID), the CDC, and the Department of Defense to lead a major intervention in West Africa to contain the epidemic. The following year, the Obama administration drew on funds remaining from this emergency allocation to make a twenty-fivefold increase in its support for the Global Health Security Agenda, pledging US$1 billion dollars toward assistance in implementing the IHR core capacities in poor countries. Like Lederberg and Frieden before him, President Obama invoked national self-interest to explain the need for US investment in other countries' health infrastructure: "promoting global health security is a core tenet of our national strategy for countering biological threats," he declared. "No single nation can be prepared if other nations remain unprepared to counter biological threats."[27] Insofar as the IHR core capacities had not yet been implemented in countries at risk of emerging disease outbreaks, the United States remained vulnerable to the spread of a novel and deadly pathogen. The president directed his National Security Council to convene an interagency committee, comprised of representatives from the State Department, the Department of Defense, the CDC, USAID and other agencies, to coordinate the work of the GHSA, under the lead of the Council's Director for Global Health Security and Biodefense, Elizabeth Cameron.

Indicators as a tool of global governance

To enact the global system of outbreak management envisioned by the Global Health Security Index, US officials sought a method to ensure that each country was progressing toward implementing its required core capacities. Obama's executive order pointed to the central role to be played by technical assessment in the GHSA's program for advancing a condition of health security: according to the executive order, the GHSA would seek "to accelerate partner countries' measurable capabilities to achieve specific targets to prevent, detect, and respond to infectious disease threats."[28] The method of assessment that the GHSA developed, in collaboration with the WHO, was called a "joint external evaluation." There were two stages to the joint evaluation process: first, a self-assessment by the national government, and then an external assessment conducted by a Joint External Evaluation (JEE) team consisting of experts from the WHO, the World Organization for Animal Health, INTERPOL, and other multilateral organizations. After a five-day presentation covering nineteen different technical areas, the JEE team would assign a numerical score for the country's capacity in each of these areas. Once compiled, the country's overall score served as a baseline to gauge future improvements.

The process of assessing a given country's overall level of "health security" raises the question: how is it possible to measure a country's ability to manage an event – a potential future outbreak – that has not yet occurred? Here is where the "indicator" came in. An indicator, as historian of science Theodore Porter explains, is a device used to point to an abstract entity, such as "the national economy," that cannot easily be grasped through direct measurement. In place of the thing of interest itself, an indicator measures "something whose movements show a consistent relation to that thing."[29] In building an index to assess this abstract entity, Porter continues, one need not inquire too deeply into the thing being measured: "Since its purpose is merely to indicate as a guide to action, ease of measurement is preferred to meaning or depth." In the case of the joint evaluation process, then, it was perhaps less important to know what exactly a condition of health security was than to generate targets – measurable capabilities – on which one could work to improve it. Indeed, one can say that it was the system of indicators that constituted a country's "health security" as a possible object of knowledge and intervention.

According to the assessment process, the evaluation team was to determine a country's score using the JEE tool, contained in a 92-page document composed almost entirely of tables of indicators.[30] The nineteen technical areas covered by the JEE tool's tables of indicators were classified according to three broad rubrics: prevent, detect, and respond. The first set of indicators covered the prevention of disease emergence:

to score well, a country required elements such as functional surveillance systems, an adequate workforce, and sufficient vaccine coverage. The second set of indicators concerned the country's capacity to detect the onset of a novel infectious disease: necessary capacities here included laboratory facilities and systems for reporting outbreaks to international authorities. And the third set of indicators focused on the country's outbreak response capacity: Did it have in place an emergency response plan? Had risks and resources been mapped? The tables of indicators in the JEE tool were laid out in a color-coded scheme that enabled evaluators to score a country's capacity in each technical area on a scale from "no capacity" to "sustainable capacity."

The role of indicators as measuring devices used for comparative technical assessment is not unique to the field of global health security. As anthropologists Richard Rottenberg and Sally Engle Merry argue, indicators serve as "a globally circulating technology that can be used to quantify, compare and rank virtually any complex field of human affairs."[31] Systems of indicators are often used in the field of international development to generate quantitative data on domains of social and economic life, providing targets for policy interventions and enabling assessment of the efficacy of such interventions. They are particularly useful to multilateral agencies and philanthropic foundations that seek to gauge the effectiveness of donor-funded programs to improve the welfare of populations in poor countries. Thus, for its *Human Development Index*, the United Nations Development Program calculates and compares average life expectancy at birth, years of schooling, and per capita income for all countries in the world, and then ranks each country according to its overall score.[32] The World Bank's *World Development Indicators* enable cross-national comparison of poverty rates, population growth, agricultural yield, military expenditures, and other factors linked to the welfare of a given national population.[33] And the "global indicator framework" used to measure progress on the United Nations' Sustainable Development Goals includes over two hundred indicators for monitoring a country's path toward sustainable development, such as improvements in rates of undernourishment, maternal mortality, and rates of infectious disease.[34]

While similar to other such indicator systems in its goal of enabling comparison across national contexts and setting targets for intervention, the Joint External Evaluation tool is distinct in that it does not seek to measure the welfare of national populations through criteria such as income, longevity, infant mortality, or rates of malnutrition. Rather than the condition of the population, it assesses an infrastructural capability: whether a national government is able to adequately detect and rapidly respond to a future disease outbreak. By generating knowledge about this capability, the index points to sites of intervention that would, in principle, improve the country's ability to manage a future outbreak before it spreads globally. And given the rationale underlying global health security – that, as Frieden put it, "a threat anywhere is a threat everywhere" – targeting such sites in poor countries would protect against the spread of emerging diseases to wealthy ones.

In a "background" section, the WHO's *Joint External Evaluation Tool* document explained how the tool was to be used: the first time a country was evaluated, the tool would "establish a baseline measurement of the country's capacity and capabilities."[35] Later evaluations of the country's health security would then be able to measure any improvements and ensure that such improvements were sustained over time. As Nuzzo and Shearer explained, the JEE tool "builds on the GHSA's focus areas to provide a standard metric by which countries can assess their current baseline capacities and measure future progress toward full development of IHR capacities."[36] Once completed, the joint evaluation process would lead to the formulation of a plan to address any remaining gaps in the evaluated country's fulfillment of the core capacities requirement. With financial and technical assistance provided via the GHSA and its partners, the assessment process would thereby help developing countries to comply with their IHR obligations.[37]

Effectively, then, the GHSA was a US-led development program that supported a range of emerging disease-related projects around the world. Examples of projects that were funded through the program included: community-based efforts in Vietnam to identify infectious disease outbreaks earlier in order to shorten response times and avert epidemics; sending Congolese contact-tracing experts to Guinea to assist with disease prevention and detection efforts; training engineers to maintain the 120-plus biosafety cabinets in Ethiopia's national laboratories; acute laboratory testing for pathogens in foodborne outbreaks in India to enable public health experts to link people with similar results; and a joint WHO–Mali Ministry of Health program for training subject experts in surveillance for viral hemorrhagic fevers, polio, and yellow fever.[38]

In many ways, the GHSA resembled the World Bank and UN approaches to development mentioned above – the use of an index to set baselines and measure improvements in targeted categories, the role of cosmopolitan technical advisors, the lure of foreign aid tethered to the production of evidence of progress – but the kinds of health capacities supported by the GHSA were distinct from those that these other development indices tended to emphasize. Take, for example, the category of "public health infrastructure." A number of observers argued, after the 2014 Ebola epidemic, that the West African countries that had been affected were "lacking in essential public health infrastructure."[39] What was meant by this term? Within the framework of more traditional development aid, one might think of targeting aid resources toward the prevention of diseases that are prevalent in the population: purchasing essential medicines, building clinics, and training health workers for dealing with conditions such as malaria, HIV/ AIDS, infant diarrheal disease, or TB. But the core capacities supported by the GHSA, following the revised International Health Regulations, embodied a very different understanding of what was meant by essential public health infrastructure. The IHR core capacities focused not on the prevention of diseases currently afflicting the population but rather on preparedness to detect and contain a future, as yet unknown emerging pathogen so that it would not spread beyond the nation's borders.

Tracking compliance

We can now trace the line from the 2014 Global Health Security Agenda to the 2019 Global Health Security Index. Like the JEE tool used by GHSA partners to assess national levels of preparedness, the GHSI was designed, as its Executive Summary explained, as a tool for the "assessment and benchmarking of health security and related capacities" among state parties to the revised IHR.[40] The indicator categories in the GHSI built on those of the JEE tool, but expanded them from seventeen to thirty-four different technical areas for assessment.[41] In following this line, we might also note that one of the co-directors of the GHSI project, Elizabeth Cameron, had been director of the National Security Council's Office of Global Health and Biodefense under President Obama, where she was "instrumental in developing and launching the Global Health Security Agenda."[42] After leaving the National Security Council (NSC) at the end of the Obama administration, Cameron took on the role of vice president for Global Biological Policy and Programs at the Nuclear Threat Initiative. Thus, we can understand the GHSI as a continuation of the Obama administration's effort – accelerated after the 2014 Ebola epidemic – to support the implementation of IHR core capacities in the developing world, an effort based, by 2019, outside of government in the world of think tanks, NGOs, and philanthropic donors.

Thus, the global health security indicator is a device for tracking a country's level of compliance with the system of outbreak management envisioned in the 2005 revision of the International Health Regulations. It is a tool of global governance – of use for donors in gauging whether their investments are leading to improvements in the core capacities that are seen as critical to achieving a condition of health security. As the authors of the GHSI put it, "over time, the GHS index will spur measurable changes in national health security and improve international capability to address" the risk of "infectious disease outbreaks that can lead to international epidemics and pandemics."[43] To say that the GHSI failed to accurately predict how well countries would respond to Covid-19, then, is to misunderstand the purpose for which the index was designed. It was a tool not for anticipating pandemic response in the future but for monitoring the progress of a certain kind of development project in the present.

Given the aims for which the GHSI was constructed, its finding that – as of October 2019 – the United States ranked highest in the world in its "readiness to deal with the threat of an epidemic or pandemic" should not be surprising. The United States was the setting, beginning in the late 1980s, for the initial constitution of the problem of global health security. And over the following two decades, the country was a leader in developing plans and procedures to address the global threat of pathogen emergence. This was the model that the GHSA sought to export. Health security, as measured by indicators, involved implementing a set of technical capacities designed with a particular scenario in mind: a future situation – perhaps like the 2003 SARS outbreak or the initial weeks of the 2014 Ebola epidemic – in which the technical ability to detect and contain the emergence of a novel pathogen at its earliest stages would make it possible to manage the outbreak before it spread catastrophically. The US ranking in the GHSI demonstrated that its core technical capacities for detecting and containing such an outbreak should serve as a model for poor countries to adopt. Covid-19, however, did not match the outbreak scenario that structured the index: easily transmissible and spreading asymptomatically, it quickly spread globally to become a pandemic. Once the disease was airborne and global, the core capacities elaborated in the revised IHR were not those needed for dealing with the complex social, economic, and biomedical challenges that Covid-19 presented. It was not so much that the GHSI had measured national levels of preparedness incorrectly as that national preparedness, as measured by the GHSI, turned out to be a solution to a different problem than the one that was posed by Covid-19.

2

Essential Workers

In October 2020, not long after a Rose Garden ceremony to honor the nomination of Amy Coney Barrett to the Supreme Court, the White House became a hotspot for Covid-19 transmission. Among the many staff members infected was Press Secretary Kayleigh McEnany, who revealed her positive diagnosis to the national press corps in a message on Twitter. In her message, she sought to project an image of heroic sacrifice. "As an essential worker," she tweeted, "I have worked diligently to provide needed information to the American people." McEnany's appropriation of the term "essential worker" was perhaps ill-advised given the Trump administration's inattention to protecting those whose occupations placed them at risk.[1] But her use of the term also pointed to the fluidity of the category of essential worker, which was generally unfamiliar before the pandemic but then became widely recognized, even if its boundaries remained unclear. When the classification was first introduced in March 2020, it was estimated that 50–60 million Americans held jobs that were designated as "essential" by the Department of Homeland Security.[2] The designation encompassed a vast array of occupations, from physicians to truck drivers, from software engineers to meat-processing plant workers.

This wide range of occupations pointed to the question of how, precisely, the category of essential worker had been delimited. The stakes of this definition were high in that the category provided states with a rationale for allowing certain industries and services to continue to operate when much of social and economic life was shut down. The federal government defined the category to include "workers who conduct a range of operations and services that are essential to continued infrastructure viability."[3] But, in practice, it could seemingly be expanded in an ad hoc fashion, as when California added recreational cannabis to its list of essential industries or when the governor of Florida declared World Wrestling Entertainment to be an essential service.[4] Controversies arose over which industries could be deemed essential, as in the National Rifle Association's legal efforts to ensure that gun shops remained open or the Trump administration's classification of teachers as "critical infrastructure workers" so that states could require them to work onsite.[5] A number of other tensions emerged around the politics of the essential: how to ensure that essential workers received adequate protection against contagion, whether to require that employers provide such workers with special compensation for heightened exposure to risk, and whether they should be prioritized in future vaccine allocation schemes.[6] For critics, the category pointed to a fundamental inequality at the heart of the US pandemic response: essential workers had no choice but to put themselves at risk, working in industries – such as meat processing, agriculture, and logistics – where they kept supply chains operational so that others might work remotely.[7] Those whose work was categorized as essential were often those whose lives were most precarious.

Despite the apparent novelty of the essential worker category, and the controversies that arose around its application, there was little discussion in the public sphere of where the category had come from or how it had made such a prominent entrance onto the pandemic scene. This chapter examines how a technique of classification that was invented in the context of national security planning became a source of subjective identification and an object of political contestation. The category of essential worker came out of a broader security framework, dating from the early Cold War, for governing collective life in a future emergency. Specifically, it derived from the practice of defining certain industrial and service sectors as elements of "critical infrastructure." While this mode of classification made possible a remarkable transformation of economic and social life at the outset of the pandemic, its narrow technical purview did not include reflection on its potential for unintended effects.

Pandemic crisis

On March 13, 2020, shortly after the World Health Organization's official declaration that Covid-19 was a pandemic, the US Department of Health and Human Services (HHS) issued a Covid-19 response plan, adapted from its 2018 *Pandemic Crisis Action Plan*. The plan pointed to the need to shift government strategy from containment of the disease to "community mitigation" once the disease had spread to multiple jurisdictions. At this stage, according to the plan, mitigation measures such as limiting social gatherings, cancelling public events, and issuing stay-at-home orders might be called for. Such measures would, as experts and officials noted, help to "flatten the curve" of disease incidence. The objective of these measures would be to sustain the functioning of the health system as well as other critical infrastructures. As the plan put it, mitigation measures were designed to "reduce the peak number of cases, which also affects availability of hospitals and functionality of infrastructure," and to "preserve the functioning of critical infrastructure and mitigate impact to the economy and functioning of society."[8] In other words, as a public health expert explained in an interview in late March, "flattening the curve keeps society going."[9]

The strategy of social distancing drew on an old technique for managing infectious disease – physical separation – but directed it toward a novel objective: preventing the health system from being overwhelmed in the short term. This meant envisioning population health as dependent upon securing the ongoing function of a system for the provision of essential health resources. Pointing to epidemiological models, public health experts argued that unless stringent measures were taken, there would not be enough hospital beds, ventilators, or medical personnel to treat the expected surge in cases. From this perspective, the key question for public officials in the spring of 2020 was how to balance the requirements of care against the availability of health resources. As epidemiologist Pia MacDonald summarized the strategy underlying the imposition of social distancing measures, including shutting down non-essential industries: "At this point, flattening the curve just means the hospitals will not be overwhelmed by a sudden influx of patients."[10]

This strategy, articulated by federal health agencies, guided decisions on social distancing measures made at the state and local level. Thus, as Covid-19 cases surged in California in early April, Governor Gavin Newsom detailed the precise number of available intensive care unit beds around the state. "Why do I start with the number 774?" he asked. "Because that's the number that I wake up to that I'm most focused on in the state of California."[11] Similarly, Governor Andrew Cuomo of New York underlined the relation between epidemiological projections and available health resources in explaining the rationale for the state's emergency health measures: "If you have high compliance [with social distancing] you're down to

75,000 COVID beds, 25,000 ventilators," whereas with low public compliance "it goes up to 110 and 37," he explained. "Because this all comes down to, at the apex, can your hospital system manage the volume of people coming into the hospital system? That's all this is about at the final analysis."[12] Thus, for the authorities charged with implementing public health response, the strategy of imposing social distancing measures, which would prove increasingly controversial as the pandemic continued, was "all about" securing the availability of essential resources so that the system of health provision would not be overwhelmed.

On March 16, 2020, three days after HHS released its adapted *Pandemic Crisis Action Plan*[13] for government agencies, the White House and the Centers for Disease Control issued a set of instructions for the public entitled "Coronavirus Guidelines for America." These guidelines laid out short-term steps to achieve the goal of flattening the epidemiological curve. Following the schema for community mitigation measures outlined in its crisis action plan, the administration announced that if members of the public engaged in practices such as self-quarantining if sick, working from home, and avoiding social gatherings, restaurants, and discretionary travel, it would require only "15 days to slow the spread" of the coronavirus. But, as the plan noted, such protective measures as the closure of workplaces held the danger of crippling functions that were essential to economic and social life. Here is where the federal government's policy concerning essential workers came in: for those who "work in a critical infrastructure industry," the administration's guidelines specified, "you have a special responsibility to maintain your normal work schedule."[14] Who were these workers? Plans were already in place to assist states in making this classification. Just three days after the federal government's "Coronavirus Guidelines" were released, the Department of Homeland Security's Cybersecurity and Infrastructure Security Agency (CISA) issued a guidance on "the identification of essential critical infrastructure workers during the Covid-19 response."[15]

The CISA guidance sought to address the question: how could one minimize social interaction to reduce the rate of infection while at the same time sustaining the operation of economic life? For the sake of "public health and safety and community well-being" during the pandemic emergency, the guidance stated, certain industries had – again – a "special responsibility to continue operations," even in the face of stay-at-home orders from public health authorities. "In the modern economy," explained the document, "reliance on technology and on just-in-time supply chains means that certain workers must be able to access certain sites, facilities, and assets in order to ensure continuity of functions." I will return below to this key term, "continuity of functions." As for the question of which workers should remain physically on site, the document listed dozens of specific occupations, classified according to sixteen different infrastructure sectors, including food and agriculture, health care and public health, transportation, and commercial facilities.

The CISA guidance on the classification of essential workers was advisory rather than directive: following the US government's distributed structure of authority for emergency response, the matter of determining actual exceptions to stay-at-home orders – that is, determining who could be required to continue working on site – was under the purview of individual states rather than the federal government. Although implementation of the guidance varied according to local political and social environments, we can look to California for an example of how essential worker policy was carried out by individual states. On March 19 – the same day as the release of the CISA guidance – Governor Gavin Newsom issued an executive order requiring "all individuals" living in the state to stay at home "except as needed to maintain continuity of operations of the federal critical infrastructure sectors" identified in the CISA guidance.[16] Given "the importance of these sectors to Californians' health and wellbeing," Newsom's order continued, those employed in these vital sectors "may continue their work" on site, despite stay-at-home orders. Of course, for employees in such sectors continuing to show up to work was not necessarily optional. In April, the federal government drew on the language of critical infrastructure protection to ensure that meat and poultry processors could "continue operations" despite high rates of coronavirus infection among workers. Closures of such facilities would "threaten the continued operation of the national meat and poultry supply chain," pronounced President Trump in an executive order, "undermining critical infrastructure during the national emergency" and putting at risk the supply of "protein for Americans."[17]

Here it is worth pausing to consider the particular vision of social life – and its vulnerabilities – that underlay these various government pronouncements. Insofar as essential worker policy was directed toward fostering what Newsom described as the "health and wellbeing" of the population in the midst of a pandemic, the policy articulated a distinctive understanding of how to promote this biopolitical aim. The policy can be contrasted with traditional public health interventions, whether sanitation and hygiene measures or biomedical techniques such as vaccination and diagnostic testing. It did not involve the production of knowledge about the effects of the disease on the population – such as its prevalence, rate of spread, or severity. Rather, the essential worker policy focused on ensuring the ongoing operation of the systems underpinning social and economic life – what the CISA guidance called "continuity of functions." As Newsom's executive order put it, the "assets, systems, and networks" of the sixteen infrastructure sectors listed in the federal guidance "are considered so vital to the United States that their incapacitation or destruction would have a debilitating effect" on security, safety, or public health. At the heart of the essential worker policy, then, was an assumption that the well-being of the collective depended on securing the continuous flow of resources through a set of vital, vulnerable systems. As Newsom proclaimed, "The supply chain must continue." While it may not have been familiar to the public, CISA's essential worker policy was not invented out of whole cloth in response to the immediate challenges of the coronavirus pandemic. Rather, the policy built on an existing framework of emergency government, one designed to ensure the continued function of critical systems in the event of catastrophe.

Securing critical infrastructure

This style of reasoning about the security of collective life can be traced, at least in part, to early twentieth-century strategic reflection on the role of the airplane in modern war. In the era of total war, in which countries mobilized entire industrial economies in a "contest of national energies," air-war strategists argued that the continuous operation of a nation's industrial-production complex – composed of power plants, rail networks, and key industrial facilities – was critical to its military power.[18] The aim of air war, according to these strategists, was therefore to disrupt the systems that were essential to the industrial economy of the enemy nation. As airpower theorist William Sherman wrote in 1926, "industry consists of a complex system of interlocking factors, each of which makes only its allotted part of the whole," and "this very quality of modern industry renders it vulnerable" to targeted attack.[19] Sherman argued that airpower should target the enemy's "system of supply" – the complex of industrial facilities, energy infrastructures, and transportation networks that underpinned a nation's military power. During World War II, economists specializing in modeling the flow of resources in an industrial economy worked with allied air-force units to put this strategy of "precision bombing" into practice.[20] In order to advise the air force on where to most effectively target air strikes, these economists developed a sophisticated method for determining the most vulnerable nodes in the enemy nation's military-industrial production complex. According to this economic approach, such factors as "cushion" and "substitutability" were key to the resilience of a given industrial production system.

In the early Cold War, defense mobilization planners in the federal government became concerned that the Soviet Union would target key industrial facilities and essential services in a future bombing attack, crippling the American war effort. To determine sites of vulnerability in need of protection, these planners transposed methods for analyzing the "complex system of interlocking factors" underpinning the flow of resources in the national economy from air targeting and industrial mobilization to domestic vulnerability analysis.[21] In turn, their mobilization plans extended beyond preparing for the military aspects of the war to encompass the post-attack management of domestic vital resources in order to ensure the survival of the national population and the nation's capacity for economic rehabilitation in the aftermath of nuclear devastation.[22] Such plans envisioned the structure of a future emergency government and listed the actions, in specific resource areas, which emergency agencies would need to take in order to ensure the nation's capacity to survive and recover from an enemy attack.

Mobilization Plan D-Minus (1957), which was developed in anticipation of a Soviet nuclear attack, can be seen as the first national emergency preparedness plan. The plan was organized according to eight "resource categories" in which emergency actions would be taken in the event of future war: telecommunications, food, housing, industrial production, manpower, raw materials, power and fuels, and transportation.[23] These resource systems could be made more resilient to a future attack through measures such as stockpiling essential supplies, the dispersal of key industrial facilities outside of cities, and hardening potential enemy targets. Cold War mobilization planners also understood that workers would be needed to operate essential services like transportation and electric power systems and to staff key industrial plants. To ensure the survival of sufficient personnel in the aftermath of a thermonuclear attack, they proposed building a national system of blast and fallout shelters and establishing large stockpiles of essential supplies, such as medicine and food. While the impetus for federal government investment in such nuclear preparedness efforts faded over the decades that followed, and the proposed nationwide shelter system was never built, this framework for emergency government – based on the idea of ensuring the continuity of essential functions – was gradually extended to address a range of other threats, including natural disasters, terrorist attacks, and eventually, pandemics.[24] The task of planning for future emergencies was assigned to a series of different federal agencies, culminating in the 1979 establishment of the Federal Emergency Management Agency, where "all-hazards planning" was instituted as the basis for preparedness.[25]

Beginning in the mid-1990s, national security experts argued that, in response to new forms of vulnerability arising from dependence on information and communications technology, the federal government should undertake a major initiative to protect the nation's "critical infrastructure." One impetus for this concern was the specter of major software glitches arising from the "Y2K bug" as the year 2000 approached. A presidential commission was charged to "study the critical infrastructures that constitute the life support systems of our nation, determine their vulnerabilities and propose a strategy for protecting them into the future."[26] In its findings, the commission drew on a central premise of Cold War thinking about the vulnerability of the nation's vital systems. "Our infrastructures," as its 1997 report put it, "are the lifelines on which we as a nation depend." Indeed, "certain of our infrastructures are so vital" that their impairment would have devastating economic and political consequences. Given this vulnerability, the commission argued, government policy must "assure the availability and continuity of the critical infrastructures on which our economic security, defense, and standard of living depend." Reducing the nation's infrastructural vulnerability would require "coordinated effort within and between the private and public sectors," and a partnership between the federal government and state and local governments. The report identified eight critical systems "whose incapacity or destruction would have a debilitating impact on our defense or economic security," a phrase that Gavin Newsom's executive order, issued 25 years later, would repeat nearly verbatim. The critical systems identified by the commission were strikingly similar to the "resource categories" that had been defined, four decades earlier, as part of mobilization planning in the early Cold War defense: telecommunications, electrical power, oil and gas, banking and finance, transportation, water supply, emergency services, and government services. Finally, the report proposed the establishment of an office in the federal government that would "[o]versee and facilitate infrastructure assurance policy formation," including risk assessment, integrating public and private-sector perspectives, and proposing new infrastructure protection measures.

The result of this initiative, the federal government's Critical Infrastructure Protection program, was eventually housed in the Department of Homeland Security (DHS), established in late 2002 in the aftermath of the terrorist attacks of September 11, 2001. In 2006, DHS published the *National Infrastructure Protection Plan,* which laid out a vision – familiar from Cold War defense mobilization – of the dependence of social and economic life on the continued operation of the nation's vital systems. "Our national well-being depends upon secure and resilient critical infrastructure – those assets, systems and networks that underpin society," as a revised version of the

DHS plan stated.[27] It warned that "[g]rowing interdependencies across critical infrastructure systems have increased the potential vulnerabilities to physical and cyber threats." Given the limited role of the federal government in regulating private-sector infrastructural systems, the plan noted, the "primary mechanism" for advancing critical infrastructure protection would be voluntary collaboration between private-sector operators and their "government counterparts."

At around this time, in the early 2000s, a new threat came to the attention of federal emergency planners: whether due to a bioterrorist attack or the naturally occurring emergence of a novel and deadly pathogen, public health and security experts argued, the nation was ill-prepared to deal with the onset of a catastrophic "biological incident." It was necessary to prepare in advance for the potential impact of such an incident on critical infrastructures. The specter of an avian influenza pandemic, which intensified in 2005 as migratory birds spread the virus globally, led to detailed reflection on how the nation's vital systems might be affected by a pandemic. As the Homeland Security Council's 2005 *National Strategy for Pandemic Influenza* put it, "[m]ovement of essential personnel, goods and services, and maintenance of critical infrastructure are necessary during an event that spans months in any given community." The national strategy charged DHS to work with private-sector operators in developing "continuity of operations plans that ensure essential services remain functional and essential goods remain available in the event of a pandemic."[28]

DHS laid out its plans for ensuring the continuity of essential operations in a future pandemic in a *Biological Incident Annex* to the *National Response Framework*, first issued in 2008. In a revised version released in 2017, the department described the annex as the "organizing framework for responding and recovering from a range of biological threats" across the federal government.[29] The *Biological Incident Annex*, along with the 2018 *Pandemic Crisis Action Plan*, would become a key reference point in early federal responses to the Covid-19 pandemic such as the March 2020 CISA guidance (described on p. 39). On the one hand, *Pandemic Crisis Action Plan* specified the social distancing measures, or "nonpharmaceutical interventions," that would be necessary to reduce the rate of disease incidence in the population. On the other hand, the *Biological Incident Annex* laid out a series of goals that would enable social and economic life to continue to function despite the imposition of social distancing measures. These objectives included securing infrastructure systems, restoring "transportation pathways to facilitate supply chains and the movement of people," and facilitating the delivery of supplies critical to response and recovery. The federal role in the pandemic response would also include "prioritization of medical countermeasure dispensing to critical infrastructure operators." However, there was no discussion, in these various planning documents, of the question – which would become so critical during the Covid-19 emergency – of how exactly states were to make decisions about the classification of essential workers.

With this background, we can understand the March 2020 federal guidance on the identification of essential workers – and in particular, its emphasis on the need "to maintain the services and functions Americans depend on daily and that need to be able to operate resiliently" during the pandemic response – not as an ad hoc response to the Covid-19 emergency but as part of a long trajectory of emergency planning in the United States, a readymade device that was structured by a distinctive form of rationality – system-vulnerability thinking. The guidance allowed for interpretive flexibility on the part of state officials, leading to a flurry of lobbying activity by operators of potentially critical infrastructures who sought to keep their businesses in operation. From the perspective of those workers classified as "essential," in turn, key questions included first, whether one had the choice *not* to be exposed to the risk of contagion, and second – if one remained on site – whether sufficient protection would be offered.[30] For those infected on the job – such as the estimated 44,000 meatpacking workers who had tested positive for coronavirus by October 2020 – there was the further question of whether treatment would be accessible or compensation offered.[31] Finally, for critical analysts, the category of the "essential" could be understood as a new form of social classification, one that interacted in complex ways with existing forms of social inequality. A mechanism that had been put in place to reduce vulnerability at the level of the system had generated a novel form of risk at the level of individuals and communities – the risk of being classified as essential.

3

The Strategic National Stockpile

In the early months of the coronavirus pandemic, the American public learned about a vast but obscure government trove of emergency health supplies known as the "Strategic National Stockpile."[1] The location and overall contents of this storehouse were kept classified for national security reasons. But some details could be gleaned from prior reports, including the existence of six huge warehouses scattered in different parts of the country. A *Washington Post* reporter who toured one of the warehouses in 2018 described it as the size of "two super Walmarts," holding thousands of shrink-wrapped boxes of medicines, stacked on shelves five stories high.[2] The Strategic National Stockpile contained roughly eight billion dollars' worth of supplies and had an annual budget of around six hundred million dollars. Managed by the US Department of Health and Human Services, its official mission was to "provide for the emergency health security of the United States." But confronted with the most severe public health emergency the country had faced over the prior century, the stockpile seemed to be failing in its mission.

As desperately ill patients flooded hospitals, health workers faced dire shortages of essential medical supplies such as personal protective gear and ventilators. Neither existing inventories nor production increases could meet the surge in demand for emergency supplies, especially since most of the needed items were produced in China, where supply chains had been interrupted by the pandemic. States vied with one another for scarce supplies as middlemen hiked prices for protective gear as much as sevenfold. Governor Cuomo of New York described the intense competition over essential equipment: "It's like being on eBay with 50 other states bidding on a ventilator."[3] Healthcare workers were forced to reuse their masks multiple times or had to resort to makeshift protections like trash bags to shield themselves from infection. As a surgeon in California commented, doctors and nurses were "at war with no ammo."[4] In other institutional settings with high risk of exposure to the coronavirus, such as nursing homes, meatpacking plants and homeless shelters, workers and residents were even less likely to be provided with protective gear. President Trump shrugged off federal responsibility for the provision of essential supplies to states and localities: "The federal government's not supposed to be out there buying vast amounts of items and then shipping."[5] An ad hoc White House operation to procure supplies from foreign sources, coordinated by the president's son-in-law, seemed only to add to the chaos.[6] By July, hundreds of healthcare workers had died from exposure to the virus, with many of these deaths attributed to inadequate protective equipment. The leader of a national organization of nurses decried the lack of help from the federal government: "It's almost five months into a pandemic in the richest country in the world and we're putting people's lives at risk because we don't have enough PPE," she lamented. "These deaths are entirely preventable."[7]

Despite its expansive scale, the Strategic National Stockpile was ill-equipped to make up for the nation's shortfall in emergency health supplies. The reserves of 12 million N95 masks that it held at the start of the pandemic were depleted by the beginning of April. Meanwhile, health officials estimated that 3.5 billion masks would be needed over the course of the pandemic. And while the stockpile did not have nearly enough emergency health supplies on hand to meet the urgent demands generated by the pandemic, there were large quantities of items in the stockpile that were not helpful in responding to Covid-19: millions of doses of smallpox vaccine, for example, as well as expansive supplies of prophylactic anthrax treatment and over a thousand caches of nerve-gas antidote. In this context, critical observers and public officials began to ask about the reasons behind the Strategic National Stockpile's apparent failure in the face of emergency: Why did the government's emergency medical storehouse lack the supplies that were essential for managing a pandemic?[8] How to explain, as a later government report put it, the "apparent mismatch between stakeholders' expectations and SNS capabilities during the COVID-19 response"?[9]

In June 2020, the Senate Committee on Homeland Security and Government Affairs sought to shed light on these questions in a hearing on "the Strategic National Stockpile and Pandemic Response."[10] The committee's ranking member, Sen. Gary Peters, framed the hearings with a stark description of the stockpile's inability to address urgent needs soon after the pandemic's onset: "the scale of the coronavirus pandemic depleted our National Stockpile in just a matter of weeks, leaving state and local governments scrambling to acquire the masks, the gloves, and other supplies that were so desperately needed in order to keep people safe." In his opening remarks, the committee chair, Sen. Ron Johnson, posed the question of how the national stockpile's mission had been defined, pointing to "a pervasive problem of lack of clarity and understanding of exactly what the SNS's role is and what it should be." As the hearing progressed, expert testimony made it clear that the stockpile had not been designed to address an event like the Covid-19 pandemic.

The hearing's first witness, former CDC director Julie Gerberding, argued that during its history the stockpile had been assigned too many different roles. Over the prior two decades, she noted, the SNS had shifted "from being something that was oriented toward bioterrorism, then to all hazards, CBRN preparation, then influenza pandemic." Another expert, the RAND Corporation's Daniel Gerstein, testified that, despite its significant budget, the federal stockpile had never been intended to deal with a nationwide public health emergency. Rather, it was envisioned as a stopgap measure to supplement local response: "neither the stockage levels nor funding were ever considered to be adequate for large-scale biological events, certainly not ones that affected all 56 states, territories, and the District of Columbia simultaneously."[11] Going forward, Gerstein argued, the stockpile's official mission should be revised in order to better "signal the capabilities and limits of the SNS." Indeed, he elaborated, the US pandemic response had "exposed critical weaknesses in the SNS," involved "a significant departure from planning, doctrine, and exercises" and had left states to "fend for themselves." These failures had contributed to an overall "loss of confidence in the federal government." As a result, he argued, it was now necessary to "reexamine the SNS concept" more generally.

Let us pause for a moment on this question of the "concept" underlying the Strategic National Stockpile. The governmental practice of assembling a storehouse of essential supplies for use in a future emergency hinges on an understanding of collective life as vulnerable to disruptive shock. The medical stockpile serves as a store of goods held on standby to provide for the health of the population in a future, post-disaster world of resource scarcity and system breakdown. At the same time, there are limits to the concept of a government-managed stockpile of essential supplies: the items in a stockpile tend to deteriorate or become obsolete, at which point they must be sold off or given away. The acquisition and maintenance of a stockpile's supplies is ever subject to budgetary struggles because it is impossible to know whether one is going to need its materials. Moreover, it may turn out – as we saw during the coronavirus pandemic – that the event for which one has planned differs so much from the one that actually occurs that the stockpile's contents are of little use. This is the temporal paradox of the stockpile: it is assembled in relation to a particular vision of the future, but that vision remains frozen in the moment of its assembly.

The Cold War medical stockpile

While there is a long history of storing supplies in preparation for a future disaster – dating as far back as the ancient Egyptian practice of grain storage to avert famine – the technical practice of government stockpiling is relatively new.[12] Government stockpiling of essential supplies began with the wartime mobilization of industrial economies. The term "stockpile" did not come into common use until the lead-up to World War II, when the United States began storing large quantities of "critical and strategic materials" – basic industrial inputs such as copper, tungsten, and rubber – in anticipation of a potential cutoff of foreign supplies.[13] The wartime US stockpiling program was from the outset conceptualized as a form of "cushion," making it possible, in advance of an anticipated interruption in the flow of key resources, to ensure the ongoing function of vital production systems. After World War II, the technique of stockpiling essential supplies to provide security against future system disruption migrated from the world of military-industrial mobilization to that of civilian protection against enemy air attack.

The adoption of a program of government stockpiling of civilian goods was motivated by the findings of the US Strategic Bombing Survey, a massive research project begun in 1944 to assess the efficacy of the WWII allied air campaign. The survey sought to address a puzzle for US air-war strategists: why had Germany's industrial economy proven surprisingly resilient to the Allies' massive air attack? Even in the later stages of the war, the survey found, the German economy had a "substantial cushion of potential production," enabling it to continue to produce weapons despite the destruction caused by the air campaign. Similarly, large inventories of essential goods "helped cushion the people of the German cities from the effects of bombing," according to the survey. Meanwhile, Germany's industrial machinery was incompletely used, and so it was "comparatively easy to substitute unused or partly used machinery for that which was destroyed."[14] Thus the existence of reserves – whether in stockpiles or as unused facilities – had been key to the German industrial economy's capacity to absorb devastating losses and yet continue to produce military goods – what the survey called its "resilience."

At the close of World War II, US national security planners were already looking ahead to the possibility of a future air attack on American cities. Following its analysis of German resilience, the Strategic Bombing Survey suggested that the vulnerability of American cities to such an attack could be "enormously decreased by a well worked out program of stockpiles, dispersal and special construction" of industrial facilities. In the late 1940s, the National Security Resources Board (NSRB), a mobilization planning agency charged with developing a strategy for US civil defense, drew on the approach advised by the Strategic Bombing Survey in considering the problem of post-attack medical treatment. The scenario of a nuclear attack presented a daunting challenge for civil defense planning. As the NSRB's Director of Health Mobilization put it, "the treatment of many thousands" of post-attack casualties presented national security planners with "enormous and unprecedented administrative and organizational difficulties."[15] To address these difficulties, NSRB officials began by conducting an investigation of the entire national system of health provision, looking at inventories, production capacity, available personnel, and the location of key facilities. The resulting study revealed key sites of vulnerability: there was no warehousing of critical medical equipment, retailers did not stock supplies beyond a short window of time, and hospitals held minimal reserves. In other words, the health system had very little cushion against a crippling disruption. A potential way to reduce the system's vulnerability, the Director of Health Mobilization suggested, was to build "necessary security reserves of health supplies."

This recommendation guided the Federal Civil Defense Administration (FCDA) in its development of a medical stockpiling program soon after its inception in 1950. The civil defense medical stockpile was designed in preparation for a large-scale nuclear attack on American cities. In the aftermath of such an attack, planners anticipated that neither existing inventories of health supplies nor increased production would be capable of addressing the population's urgent medical needs. The government's ability to address these needs would depend on actions that had been taken well in advance of the event: the purchase and storage of sufficient supplies as well as the development of a plan for their rapid distribution. Based on an initial calculation of available medical personnel, FCDA proposed a goal of stockpiling enough supplies to treat an estimated "casualty load" of five million survivors over a period of three weeks after the attack. These supplies would be dispersed "in strategic spots throughout the United States," outside of urban centers but close enough to be accessible to mobile populations fleeing attacks on cities.[16] The agency requested US$400 million from Congress to build its envisioned medical stockpile but received only a third of this amount – a pattern that would be repeated as the civil defense stockpiling program limped forward over the following years.

The nucleus of the Cold War medical stockpile was the two-hundred bed "civil defense emergency hospital," stored in crates and designed to be rapidly assembled within any available structure, such as a school or a church. Each packaged emergency hospital had an inventory of 690 different items, including pharmaceuticals and surgical supplies, as well as equipment to generate electricity and pump water in an envisioned future of infrastructural breakdown. These items were stored in 485 separate crates, weighing a total of 25 tons. In order to treat "the great casualty load anticipated in an all-out attack," FCDA calculated that it would need to maintain some six thousand of these hospitals available in dispersed locations, but due to budget shortfalls the stockpile had acquired less than two thousand of them by 1957. During a brief period of congressional enthusiasm for civil defense in 1962, FCDA was allocated funds for the purchase of an additional 750 of the packaged hospitals, but in the following years there was little support for either the acquisition of more emergency supplies or the maintenance and care of existing ones. Out-of-date drugs were not replaced, the safety and sterility of equipment was not ensured. The civil defense medical stockpile was both increasingly obsolete and too expensive to upgrade. By the end of the decade, hundreds of millions of dollars' worth of unused medical supplies were gradually deteriorating in storage facilities around the country.

A humanitarian experiment

At around this time, the civil defense medical stockpile was used in an unexpected way. The context was a widely publicized humanitarian emergency unfolding in West Africa. Beginning in 1968, the Nigerian military's siege of Biafra led to mass starvation and to urgent international calls for intervention. As part of an airlift of relief supplies coordinated by US religious groups and supported by the Nixon administration, the US Agency for International Development shipped thirteen of the FCDA stockpile's packaged emergency hospitals to Nigeria. An official from the US Public Health Service named Robert Price accompanied one of the packaged hospitals to its final destination in Port Harcourt on the southern coast of the country, with the mission to "advise and assist" the Nigerians in setting up and using it.[17]

In a report published in 1970, Price described the situation upon his arrival in Port Harcourt, where the existing general hospital served as a "haven" for sick and injured victims of the civil war but had no equipment or supplies for treating patients' maladies, which ranged from gunshot wounds to malnutrition to malaria. Price noted in his report that the packaged emergency hospitals, stowed away in dispersed locations and intended for the aftermath of a nuclear attack, had never been fully put to use. The conflict in Nigeria, he wrote, "provided the first real opportunity to use these units in their entirety and to assess the usefulness of the concept" of the packaged disaster hospital.[18] For Price, the unprovisioned general hospital in Port Harcourt was a setting in which to test how the stockpiled emergency health supplies would function in what he called "the hostile environment" of a post-nuclear attack United States – that is, a situation of infrastructural collapse in which victims of catastrophe desperately needed medical care.

Price reported on the result of the stockpile experiment in West Africa: while there were certain health needs in Port Harcourt that the packaged equipment and supplies could not address, such as drugs for parasitic disease, his assessment was that it had overall been a success. The hospital was assembled rapidly, its wheeled cots and other equipment functioned well, and stored supplies like intravenous recipient kits had saved the lives of badly malnourished children. The "experience in Nigeria," Price concluded, demonstrated the more general "usefulness of the concept of a packaged, quickly activated hospital" and justified "the modest expense necessary to maintain readiness to respond to disaster."[19]

The flexibility of the packaged emergency hospital had made it translatable to a very different setting than the one for which it had been commissioned. But Price's demonstration of its utility in the context of humanitarian emergency was not enough to garner continued congressional support for the civil defense stockpiling program. It was difficult to command sustained investment to maintain ongoing readiness for an event that might never occur. As Price was writing, civil defense was rapidly falling out of favor. Just three years after his report appeared, in 1973, the stockpiling program was cancelled for budgetary reasons, and its trove of supplies was quietly disposed of.[20] One might say that the career of the packaged disaster emergency hospital, and the civil defense medical stockpile more generally, reached its modest apogee in Port Harcourt, in the first (and last) time it was fully put into practice. But the concept of stockpiling essential supplies for a future health emergency did not go away: it was renewed three decades later in a very different context of perceived risk.

A novel threat

In the late 1990s, national security officials in the Clinton administration became concerned about the whereabouts of large stocks of biological weapons such as anthrax and smallpox that the Soviet Union had accumulated during the Cold War.[21] In particular, they worried that such bioweapons had fallen into the hands of a rogue nation or terrorist group that could launch a biological attack against the United States. The perceived urgency of this threat was heightened by President Clinton's encounter with a work of fiction: a novel by science journalist Richard Preston called *The Cobra Event,* which told the story of a catastrophic bioweapons attack using an engineered variant of smallpox.[22] Alarmed by Preston's vision, Clinton called together administration officials and biosecurity experts to provide counsel on how to address what seemed to be an imminent threat for which the United States was dangerously unprepared.[23] The resulting articulation of the biosecurity problem – and its potential solution – would guide the construction and maintenance of the Strategic National Stockpile over the next two decades, leading up to the coronavirus pandemic.

As national security experts conceptualized it, the key problem posed by the threat of a biological attack concerned the immediate availability of medical countermeasures. In the aftermath of such an attack, as they envisioned it, there would be an urgent need for the rapid distribution of drugs or vaccines effective against the weaponized pathogen. This need could not be addressed by the existing system of health provision since, absent the prevalence of the disease in the population, there was no market for pharmaceutical products targeted against likely bioweapons such as smallpox and anthrax. The only way to mitigate this vulnerability would be for the federal government to procure and store such countermeasures in advance of an attack.[24] Thus, a stockpile of medical countermeasures would accomplish what the market could not: ensure the availability of a supply of essential medical supplies to be rapidly distributed to the population in the event of a public health emergency. In 1999, Congress provided an emergency allocation to the Centers for Disease Control to establish the National Pharmaceutical Stockpile, in order to counter "potential biological, disease and chemical threats to civilian populations."[25]

As during the Cold War, in order to calculate stockpile requirements it was necessary to estimate the post-attack needs of the population in the absence of historical experience of the event to be planned for. Officials drew on simulated attacks to determine the medical supplies that would be needed and to generate congressional support for the allocation of funds to acquire them. In June 2001, two Washington, DC-based think tanks hosted a scenario-based exercise called "Dark Winter" at Andrews Air Force Base in Maryland, in which a group of current and former public officials participated.[26] The exercise began with a bioterrorist attack involving the release of smallpox virus in multiple locations. According to the scenario for the exercise, local public health responders could not contain the spread of the disease due to a shortage of smallpox vaccine, leading to thousands of deaths, widespread civil unrest, and finally to political breakdown as states contested with one another over dwindling vaccine supplies. The outcome pointed to a specific vulnerability: the lack of sufficient smallpox vaccine on hand in advance of an attack. Afterward, the organizers of the exercise held briefings on its findings with members of Congress and the executive branch. One result was the procurement of enough doses of smallpox vaccine for the National Pharmaceutical Stockpile to inoculate the entire US population, at an estimated cost of US$500 million – an amount that would continue to grow over time, given the considerable cost of storing the vaccine and replacing expired doses.[27]

Later that year, the terrorist attacks of September 11 and the anthrax letters that followed led to further government investment in biosecurity. In June 2002, Congress passed the Public Health Security and Bioterrorism Preparedness and Response Act. Among other provisions, the legislation changed the name of the pharmaceutical stockpile to the "Strategic National Stockpile," expanding its scope and contents. It was left to the discretion of the Secretary of Health and Human Services to determine which supplies were "appropriate and practicable" to be added to the stockpile.[28] Two years later, Congress enacted Project BioShield, which allocated US$5.6 billion over ten years to the Department of Health and Human Services for the purchase of countermeasures against biological threats, such as anthrax and smallpox, to be stored in the

Strategic National Stockpile.[29] Project BioShield charged the Department of Homeland Security (DHS) to determine which material threats should be addressed by the stockpile program.

However, it proved difficult for stockpile managers to acquire countermeasures against the threat agents identified by DHS in that established drugmakers were reluctant to invest in the lengthy and expensive process of drug development, given the lack of an existing market. Another piece of legislation, the 2006 Pandemic and All-Hazards Preparedness Act, addressed this "gap in advanced research and development" through the establishment of the Biomedical Advanced Research and Development Agency (BARDA) within the Department of Health and Human Services (HHS).[30] The idea was that the new agency would contract with biotech and pharmaceutical firms for the delivery of future medicines and would help steer potential treatments through the research and development process. The 2006 legislation also created an office of the Assistant Secretary for Preparedness and Response, which would oversee BARDA and coordinate the Strategic National Stockpile. And, finally, the legislation established the Public Health Emergency Medical Countermeasures Enterprise (PHEMCE), an interagency body whose task would be to determine which countermeasures should be pursued to address the material threats identified by DHS. Over the next several years, the federal government signed a series of lucrative contracts with biotech firms to develop supplies for the stockpile. Some of these led to accusations of cozy relationships between drug industry lobbyists and stockpile managers – for instance, a multiyear contract signed by BARDA with Emergent BioSolutions for a novel anthrax vaccine.[31]

During this period, the stockpile program began to expand its purview beyond countermeasures against bioweapon threats. As the H5N1 avian influenza virus circulated globally among migratory birds, experts warned that the virus could mutate to become more easily transmissible among humans, potentially sparking a catastrophic pandemic. In response, the White House developed a *National Strategy for Pandemic Influenza* (2005), which included the goals of stockpiling antiviral medication and improving domestic influenza vaccine-production capacity. Over the next two years, HHS purchased tens of millions of doses of the antiviral medications Tamiflu and Relenza for the Strategic National Stockpile.[32] While the feared avian influenza pandemic did not materialize, a pandemic caused by a less virulent strain of flu did occur. During the 2009 H1N1 (swine flu) pandemic, the Strategic National Stockpile drew on a one-time supplemental allocation from Congress to acquire and distribute 85 million N95 masks. Since the supply of masks had been purchased using an emergency supplemental allocation, it was never replenished, especially as pandemic influenza faded as a priority in the aftermath of H1N1. This would become a source of recrimination a decade later at the outset of the Covid-19 pandemic.

The problem of need

The supplies that are stored in the Strategic National Stockpile can be placed into two broad categories. First, there are items that can be used for a range of potential events, and which are typically available in inventories or on the market, but which might become scarce in an emergency: for instance, ventilators, N95 masks, and syringes. This category also includes the supplies contained in "federal medical stations": medicine, equipment, and beds that – like the Cold War packaged emergency hospitals – can be used to turn a pre-identified building into a temporary medical center. Other supplies with a range of potential uses are the materials, such as antibiotics and oxygen tubing, stored in "push packages," ready to be shipped to an affected city or region.[33] The second category is made up of supplies that would only be needed in a specific scenario, but for which there is no existing market (since the condition in question is not prevalent) and so a government stockpile program is the only way to ensure availability if the need arises. Many of these supplies are expensive to procure and complicated to store. This category includes items such as anthrax treatments, doses of smallpox vaccine, botulism antitoxin (which must be stored at −4° Fahrenheit), caches of nerve-gas antidote (which are stored in 1,300 different locations to enable rapid distribution), and treatment for radiation poisoning.

In the years leading up to the Covid-19 pandemic, the managers of the Strategic National Stockpile continued to prioritize supplies in the latter category, which addressed the specific threat agents – such as smallpox and anthrax – that had initially prompted the stockpile's establishment. Thus, between 2015 and 2019, countermeasures against smallpox and anthrax alone accounted for roughly three-quarters of SNS spending.[34] This emphasis accelerated in the first three years of the Trump administration. In 2017, biodefense specialist Robert Kadlec was appointed as Assistant Secretary for Preparedness and Response. As a Senate staffer, Kadlec had played a central role in drafting the 2006 legislation that established BARDA and the office of the Assistant Secretary of Preparedness and Response (ASPR). He had long voiced skepticism about the need to incorporate naturally occurring diseases such as influenza into stockpile planning. As he testified in 2011, "Mother Nature is not a thinking enemy intent on inflicting grievous harm to our country, killing our citizens, undermining our government or destroying our way of life."[35] In the years before taking on the role of assistant secretary, Kadlec led a consulting firm that advised pharmaceutical companies, such as Emergent BioSolutions, on strategies for contracting with HHS to develop medical countermeasures against bioweapons.[36] In 2018, now in charge of the preparedness office within HHS, Kadlec announced that Emergent, which had recently acquired the rights to a smallpox vaccine from the government's previous supplier, Sanofi-Pasteur, had been awarded a ten-year, US$2.8 billion contract to provide the Strategic National Stockpile with additional smallpox vaccine. The following year, Kadlec's office signed a US$535 million contract with Emergent for the stockpile to purchase a product to treat the side effects caused by the smallpox vaccine, and the office also extended a US$260 million option on an existing contract with Emergent for anthrax vaccine.[37]

It was not that anthrax and smallpox were, in 2018 and 2019, newly considered to be significant national security threats. Rather, these pathogens were a long-standing part of the threat portfolio that the stockpile had been charged to address. It remained plausible to make the case, as Kadlec did in announcing Emergent's ten-year contract with HHS for smallpox vaccine, that "[t]he virus remains a potential threat to national and global health security," and therefore, that "[h]aving vaccines and treatments at the ready will be imperative to saving lives." We might note that the stockpile was already well supplied with smallpox vaccine: according to the CDC, it contained enough to inoculate every American. But, as Kadlec argued – drawing on the rationale for the government stockpile as a substitute for market demand – ongoing purchases of the vaccine would "keep the production base warm." A renewed government contract was needed to ensure that "you have a sustainable supply, God forbid you ever need it."[38]

Kadlec's gesture toward the possibility of a future need points to a tension at the heart of the stockpile concept. In a world with an array of potential threats but finite resources to address them, what event should one be planning for? What might one need in the uncertain future? The possibilities are limited only by the imagination of security officials and by the willingness of Congress to support their requests. Unlike the civil defense medical stockpile three decades earlier, the Strategic National Stockpile had a powerful constituency for the continual update of its inventory: the world of biosecurity contractors and lobbyists. As of 2019, it seemed that the Strategic National Stockpile's priorities had not changed significantly since its establishment during the Clinton administration. The billions of dollars spent on smallpox and anthrax vaccines over the two decades before the Covid-19 pandemic point to the rigidity of the stockpile concept: up until 2020, it remained focused on the threats that animated its establishment in 1999. Because its contents were classified, and decisions on what to stockpile were at the discretion of the HHS Secretary, there had never been much public discussion – until the coronavirus pandemic – of whether the stockpile was concentrating on the right threats. While the PHEMCE made recommendations on stockpiling decisions based on confidential threat assessments from the Department of Homeland Security, it is not clear the extent to which stockpile managers were bound to follow these recommendations. In any case, upon taking on the role of ASPR, Kadlec sidelined the PHEMCE in a reorganization.

In the spring of 2020, as the Strategic National Stockpile ran short of urgently needed supplies such as personal protective equipment, the previously obscure question of how decisions had been made on the stockpile's contents suddenly burst into public view. Kadlec was called to testify before Congress concerning the stockpile's failure to have on hand sufficient emergency supplies, such as N95 masks and ventilators, in the first months of the pandemic. In his testimony, Kadlec acknowledged that stockpile managers had not been focused on what supplies, beyond drugs or vaccines, might be needed in the event of a pandemic caused by a novel respiratory disease for which there were no available pharmaceutical interventions. "We did not consider a situation like this today. We thought about vaccines. We thought about therapeutics. We never thought about respirators being our first and only line of defense for health-care workers."[39] As a government report later concluded, the stockpile was "known to have enough smallpox vaccine for a nationwide vaccination campaign, but it was less prepared at the beginning of the COVID-19 pandemic for universal infectious disease countermeasures such as N95 respirators and other personal protective equipment."[40] In other words, stockpile managers had been planning for a different kind of event than the one that actually occurred.

The Strategic National Stockpile's shortcomings in the early stages of the Covid-19 pandemic point to the limitations of storing essential supplies as a means to provide security. Filled with a wide range of countermeasures against possible threats, the stockpile did not, as it turned out, contain enough of what was needed to address the event that actually occurred. The official mission of the Strategic National Stockpile was extensive – to provide "emergency health security" – but in a world of limited resources, the critical question remained: security against what? Two decades after the formation of the Strategic National Stockpile, biosecurity planners remained committed to the aging vision of the future – post-Cold War anxiety about an impending biological attack – that had shaped its initial formation.

4

The Scenario-Based Exercise

During the White House Coronavirus Task Force's daily press briefing on March 19, 2020, reporters questioned President Trump about the federal government's seemingly flat-footed response to the pandemic. Why was it still so difficult for Americans to be tested for the virus?, they asked. And why did frontline health workers still lack desperately needed protective gear? "Nobody knew there would be a pandemic or epidemic of this proportion," protested the president. "Nobody has ever seen anything like this before." In response to the question of how he planned to increase the supply of essential medical items, the president again insisted that the demands generated by the pandemic had been inconceivable in advance of the event: "nobody in their wildest dreams would have ever thought that we'd need tens of thousands of ventilators."[1] The lack of foreknowledge, he implied, absolved his administration of responsibility for its failures.

These claims were soon contested by journalistic accounts that cited a series of plans, exercises, and reports that had envisioned a future pandemic and pointed to gaps in preparedness that needed to be addressed. Experts inside and outside of the government had, it seemed, anticipated just such an eventuality. For instance, a large-scale test exercise called "Crimson Contagion" had been conducted by the Trump administration's own Department of Health and Human Services (HHS) just six months earlier, in August 2019. Crimson Contagion simulated a deadly pandemic caused by a novel strain of the H7N9 avian influenza virus. In a post hoc report on the exercise, HHS officials had laid out multiple shortcomings in governmental preparedness revealed by the experience. Moreover, according to commentators in early 2020, the results of Crimson Contagion had foreshadowed many of the critical problems that were at that moment unfolding in real life: officials jockeyed over which federal agency should lead the government's response, health authorities struggled to secure essential supplies, and local officials challenged federal guidelines on business and school closures.[2]

Crimson Contagion was not the only recent test exercise that had revealed vulnerabilities to a future disease emergency. In October 2019, the Johns Hopkins Center for Health Security, in collaboration with the Bill and Melinda Gates Foundation and the World Economic Forum, held a tabletop exercise called "Event 201" that simulated the emergence of a novel bat coronavirus that became transmissible from person to person, leading to a severe pandemic. In its report on the exercise, the Center for Health Security recommended the establishment of an international stockpile of medical countermeasures including antivirals and vaccines. A year and a half earlier, the same center had hosted "Clade X," which enacted the intentional release and catastrophic spread of a laboratory-engineered virus.[3] The post hoc assessment of the exercise pointed to the need for a "strong and sustainable global health security system" as well as a "robust highly capable national public health system" to mitigate the vulnerabilities revealed by the exercise. And in January 2017, the National Security Council held a pandemic simulation for incoming Trump administration officials featuring the emergence of a novel strain of the H9N2 avian influenza virus. Lessons from this exercise included the likelihood of shortages in essential medical supplies and the need to ensure a coordinated, unified national response during a future pandemic emergency.[4]

In addition to citing such exercises, critics of the federal government's response to Covid-19 also pointed to reports that had been released in the aftermath of real-life events whose recommendations had been ignored by the current administration, such as the National Security Council's "lessons learned" study on the US response to the 2014 Ebola epidemic in West Africa. The 2016 NSC report had led to the establishment of a Directorate of Global Health Security and Biodefense within the National Security Council, which put together a "pandemic playbook" to guide early response to a "high consequence-emerging disease threat" with the potential to cause a pandemic. However, the Directorate was disbanded in 2018 as part of a reorganization of the NSC by Trump's National Security Advisor, John Bolton, and its playbook was shelved.[5]

If the aim of these earlier exercises and assessments had been to stimulate future preparedness efforts, the retrospective discussion of their findings had a different purpose: to pinpoint sites of blame for a cascading series of failures in the government's current response to Covid-19. According to journalistic accounts of the earlier exercises, their lessons had been ignored by authorities: "a cascade of warnings went unheeded," as a *New York Times* headline put it. Such accounts drew on the experience of past exercises to pose the question of where responsibility for failure lay in the present. As an August 2020 commentary in *Nature* asked, "What went wrong? Why did dozens of simulations, evaluations and white papers fail to predict or defend against the colossal missteps taken in the world's wealthiest nation?" Earlier expert recommendations based on the results of these exercises, the authors concluded, "didn't actually drive policymakers to prioritize and fund improvements to the public health system."[6]

In a similar vein, former government officials drew on the findings of prior exercises and reports to criticize the current administration's failures to follow expert advice. Writing in March 2020, former National Security Advisor Susan Rice recalled the pandemic exercise that the National Security Council had conducted with incoming Trump administration officials during the 2017 presidential transition, noting that "like much of the assistance we offered, it was discarded by the incoming team." Blame for the country's escalating failure in response to Covid-19 lay at the current president's door, argued Rice: "Rather than heed the warnings, embrace the planning and preserve the structures and budgets that had been bequeathed to him, the president ignored the risk of a pandemic."[7] Similarly, a former National Security Council official who had composed the Obama administration's "lessons learned" report on the federal government's Ebola response pointed to the "three-pronged strategy" the Obama administration had developed to "contain a more dangerous outbreak" in the future. The strategy included establishing the Directorate for Global Health Security and Biodefense, building out a network of hospitals and testing centers designated to treat Ebola, and investing a billion dollars of Ebola emergency funds into the Global Health Security Agenda. "It will never be known," argued the former official, "how much better prepared the nation and the world might have been for a coronavirus pandemic had the infrastructure called for by policymakers who fought Ebola been fully built."[8]

In its assumption of the relation between present advice and future responsibility, this pattern of critique followed a familiar narrative arc: the divinatory sign that is ignored at deadly cost, or the oracle whose prophecies of doom go unheeded, leading to catastrophe. But, as this chapter will suggest, such interpretations misread the function of administrative tools like the scenario-based exercise and the post hoc report. Rather than making claims about how to avoid future calamity, such tools are more narrowly focused on the present. They seek to make specific, and often modest, interventions into the administrative world they inhabit, and so it is perhaps unsurprising that their effects on the future may be limited.

Responsibility for the future

Such critical commentary on unheeded warnings, in its attempt to locate a site of blame for failure, is symptomatic of a broader process through which government has come to be seen as responsible for managing the consequences of a range of potential future events. Here it is helpful to draw on sociologist Niklas Luhmann's analysis of the attribution of blame for the occurrence of unfortunate events. Luhmann makes a distinction between "risk" and "danger" as two ways that a potential future loss can be conceptualized in the present. To conceive of the possible occurrence as a danger is to consider it to have been caused by an external, uncontrollable force. To consider it as a risk, on the other hand, means that its occurrence is seen as the consequence of a decision: "we can speak of risk only if we can identify a decision without which the loss could not have occurred."[9] According to Luhmann, modern societies tend to experience the future in terms of risk: "there are no longer any dangers that are strictly externally attributable," he writes. A catastrophic earthquake may strike – but we should have better reinforced our buildings given what we knew about seismic risk in the region. A destructive flood may occur – but action should have been taken to strengthen the levee system or to restrict construction in the floodplain.

The predominant approach to regulation in this arena involves the quantitative risk assessment. Such a calculation depends upon the existence of a record of past incidence to guide estimates of future risk. Drawing on historical data, a bureau charged with flood control can determine the required height of a proposed dam based on a calculation of the costs of dam construction in relation to the probability of losses that would be caused by a catastrophic flood. Or an agency charged with drug regulation may look at clinical trial data on therapeutic outcomes to compare the benefits of a drug's effects against its risk of side effects. However, the prospect of a rare or unprecedented event – for example, a nuclear reactor meltdown or a mass-casualty terrorist attack – challenges the calculative framework of risk assessment insofar as it is difficult to construct an historical pattern of incidence.[10] How, then, can government take responsibility for managing the risk of such events?

This is where a key tool of emergency planning – the scenario-based exercise – comes into play. Unlike a quantitative risk assessment, the scenario-based exercise is not based on a statistical calculation of the probability of the event's occurrence; rather, the exercise generates knowledge about vulnerabilities to a potential future event that provide officials with targets for intervention in the present.[11] This background helps us to understand the aims of the various test exercises, such as Crimson Contagion, that were held in the years before the coronavirus pandemic. The question is not so much whether these simulations anticipated the future occurrence of an event like Covid-19, but rather what vulnerabilities the exercises sought to reveal. Here it is important to consider the purposes for which a given scenario-based exercise has been organized. The aims of such exercises are typically fairly narrow: they seek to galvanize specific interventions into a particular administrative arena.[12] To understand the type of responsibility generated by the scenario-based exercise, it will be helpful to sketch its history as a planning technique.

The invention of the scenario-based exercise

The scenario-based exercise was invented in the early Cold War as a means of planning for an unprecedented future catastrophe – a nuclear attack on the United States. During this period, the Office of Defense Mobilization (ODM) within the executive branch was charged with the task of preparing for such an attack.[13] To develop a plan for governmental preparedness, ODM officials asked: what capacities would be needed to enable population survival and economic recovery in the aftermath of an attack? And what form of organization would be appropriate for administering these efforts? Given the unprecedented nature of such an event, the past could not serve as a guide for mobilization planners' efforts. ODM therefore developed scenarios of how a future attack might unfold, drawing on novel computer simulation techniques to map where bombs would strike and the damage they would inflict on key resources and concentrations of population.

The plan ODM eventually developed, *Mobilization Plan D-Minus* (1957), began with the post-attack reorganization of government.[14] According to the plan, upon the president's declaration of a wartime emergency, a series of new government agencies would come into being. An Office of War Resources would be at the apex of the new organization, coordinating the allocation of resources across existing federal agencies as well as newly formed emergency agencies such as the War Communication Administration, the War Food Administration, and the War Transport Administration. The plan charged each agency with broad areas of responsibility, outlining a series of "emergency action steps" that the agency would have to carry out upon the declaration of emergency. The bulk of *Mobilization Plan D-Minus* was composed of these emergency action steps, arrayed in lengthy tables that listed each action step, the point at which the step would have to be taken, and which agency was responsible for it. The Agriculture

Department, for example, was assigned to implement a system of food rationing and to allocate limited food supplies. The Federal Civil Defense Administration was charged to provide for the shelter needs of the population and put in place programs to meet these needs.

As part of its preparedness program, ODM developed a method for testing the ability of government agencies to perform their assigned functions in a future wartime emergency: a program of scenario-based exercises.[15] Mobilization planners conceived of these test exercises as "a continuous and effective way of enlisting and applying brainpower to the many ramifications of an unknown problem."[16] The exercise was part of an iterative planning technique in which the outcome of a given exercise would guide the revision of existing plans. Thus, a 1957 ODM memorandum explained that the goal of an upcoming exercise was "to determine what aspects of our preparedness program need greatest emphasis during the next 12 months."[17] Indeed, ODM officials planned each exercise with specific preparedness problems in mind.

In collaboration with the Federal Civil Defense Administration, ODM organized a series of large-scale governmental preparedness exercises, called "Operation Alert," beginning in 1955.[18] In designing these exercises, a key question for ODM planners concerned the organization of government authority in a post-attack situation. Who would direct the provision of relief to civilians? What would be the relation of the federal government to the states? And what role would the military play in case of a breakdown in civilian order? From the perspective of ODM's Plans and Readiness division, which oversaw the organization of the exercise, the post-attack "chain of command" would have to be planned in advance if authorities were to "cope with the indescribable chaos of a nuclear attack."[19]

When the first Operation Alert exercise was conducted in June 1955, its outcome apparently came as a surprise to its organizers. The scenario began with a massive Soviet attack on US cities. Upon being informed of the attack, President Eisenhower did not follow the planned scheme for a civilian-led chain of command. Instead, he immediately declared a state of "limited martial law" to enable the military to take command over the provision of relief to survivors. The president assumed that in the aftermath of an enemy nuclear attack, existing civil defense plans would rapidly go out the window and so military authority would be required to maintain civilian order. Eisenhower's declaration provoked widespread controversy, not least among the state and local officials who had been charged with civil defense responsibilities and were sidelined by the proclamation of martial law. Findings from the exercise were then folded back into the mobilization planning process. As a later report on the "lessons learned" from Operation Alert noted, the 1955 exercise had demonstrated the need to clarify the relation between civilian and military authority in a wartime emergency: "planning for military assistance to civil authority must be further developed" and "substitutes for martial law, if any, must be explored." In addition, the report recommended that future exercises focus on extending ODM's planning framework to states and localities "to get emergency planning out to the field more generally, so it will be prepared to act in accordance with national policy."[20]

The Cold War program of scenario-based exercises thus sought to make preparedness for nuclear war a testable – and thereby improvable – condition. Equipped with the details of a potential attack and a list of required actions, and having enrolled participants from across government, mobilization planners could assess the effectiveness of agencies' response to the enactment and then draw on lessons learned from the experience to inform future preparations. The exercise was, then, not so much an attempt to anticipate the future as it was a means, as one ODM planner put it, to "insure continuously improved mobilization plans."[21] Of course, the question of whether such improvements meant that the resulting plans would prove effective in the aftermath of an actual nuclear attack was, fortunately, never tested.

From nuclear attack to pandemics: the migration of emergency preparedness

This iterative approach to planning for an unprecedented future event – including organizational schemes, checklists of action steps, test exercises and post hoc assessments – gradually migrated from the specific context of nuclear attack preparedness to address an expansive category of "emergency." An early step in this direction was the *National Plan for Emergency Preparedness*, released in 1964 by the Office of Emergency Planning, a successor organization to ODM within the Executive Branch.[22] Like *Mobilization Plan D-Minus*, the *National Plan* was organized according to a series of resource areas – such as food, energy, fuel, and health – in which government agencies would have to take emergency actions, with the key difference that the 1964 plan applied not only to nuclear attack but to "any threat to the national security." As such plans delineating governmental responsibilities in a future emergency were tested and revised over the following decades, they branched out to address other potential threats, including natural disasters, terrorist attacks, and environmental catastrophes.[23] In turn, government agencies conducted scenario-based exercises to test their ability to meet the responsibilities spelled out in the plans. The federal government eventually consolidated numerous emergency plans into a single, unified plan, the *National Response Plan*, released in 2004 by the Federal Emergency Management Agency (FEMA), a descendant of the Office of Defense Mobilization of the 1950s and the Office of Emergency Planning of the 1960s.

Beginning in the early 2000s, US public health and national

security officials sought to incorporate the threat of infectious disease into the governmental framework of emergency preparedness. Scenario-based exercises were integral to this process. For instance, the influential 2001 Dark Winter exercise simulated the aftermath of a bioterrorist attack using weaponized smallpox.[24] According to the scenario for the exercise, the attack on an immunologically naive population upended the public health system and led to widespread political chaos. Among the gaps revealed by the Dark Winter exercise was the need to assign a single federal agency to lead the government response to a biological attack. Three years later, FEMA's *National Response Plan* charged the Secretary of Health and Human Services with operational control of public health and medical response to a biological incident under the rubric of "Emergency Support Function #8."

This concern with governmental response to a biological emergency soon extended from the threat of bioweapons to that of emerging disease, as the reemergence of H5N1 avian influenza alerted US health officials to the potential for a catastrophic flu pandemic. According to the White House's 2005 *National Strategy for Pandemic Influenza*, managing the response to such an event should not "be viewed as a purely federal responsibility," and so "the nation must have a system of plans at all levels of government and in all sectors outside of government that can be integrated to address the pandemic threat."[25] In 2006, Congress passed the Pandemic and All-Hazards Preparedness Act, which established the office of the Assistant Secretary for Preparedness and Response (ASPR) within the Department of Health and Human Services. ASPR, in turn, was charged with planning a "National Health Security Strategy," including the organization of preparedness exercises. In parallel, FEMA incorporated biological threats into federal emergency preparedness, releasing a "Biological Incident Annex" to its *National Response Framework* in 2008.

Crimson Contagion

We can now return to the series of pandemic exercises held just before the onset of Covid-19. In August 2019, the Exercise, Evaluation and After Action Division within HHS coordinated the Crimson Contagion exercise. Crimson Contagion was designed to test the federal government's most recent biological preparedness plans: the 2017 *Biological Incident Annex* to the Federal Interagency Operations Plan, and the 2018 *Pandemic Crisis Action Plan*. The central issues to be addressed by the exercise resembled those that had animated Operation Alert in 1955: how to distribute governmental responsibility for managing a future event that would present novel challenges for the organization of response. As ASPR put it in its later report on Crimson Contagion, one of its "overarching exercise objectives" was to test how the various government agencies that would be involved in a pandemic response would coordinate "protective actions" in accordance with existing plans and procedures.[26] The exercise was designed to reveal the adjustments to existing plans that were needed in order to ensure a coherent national response.

The scenario for the exercise depicted a novel strain of H7N9 avian influenza that first emerged in China and then spread rapidly around the world through air travel. At the outset of the exercise, according to the time frame detailed in the scenario, it had been 47 days since the detection of the first case of H7N9 in China. By this time, the World Health Organization had officially recognized the spread of the disease as a pandemic, and the US government had declared a national public health emergency. At a "master cell" established by the Department of Health and Human Services in Washington, DC, representatives from nineteen different federal agencies, twelve state governments, and dozens of local health departments, hospitals and private-sector organizations participated in coordinating the governmental response. Meanwhile, emergency operations centers were activated by state and local governments, NGOs, HHS, CDC, and the DHS/FEMA National Response Coordination Center.

As in the nuclear preparedness exercises of the 1950s, a central part of the iterative planning process involved garnering "lessons learned" from the exercise. Indeed, ASPR integrated the post hoc assessment process into the conduct of the exercise itself: as the event took place, participants filled out evaluation logs, after-action analysis forms, and evaluation guides. ASPR's later assessment of the performance of the exercise focused on how well each of the government's sixteen "core capabilities" for pandemic response – such as infrastructure systems, situational assessment, public information and warning, and operational coordination – had functioned. In compiling its post hoc report, the exercise evaluation team constructed a picture of participants' actions and decisions in order to identify "high level, cross-cutting issues" among the range of stakeholders involved.

ASPR's after-action report on Crimson Contagion, released in January 2020, focused on three administrative problem areas that had been exposed by the exercise and that, according to the agency, should be the object of future planning: statutory authority, coordination among disparate federal agencies, and federal–state relations.[27] The report argued that insofar as HHS was expected to take the lead in a federal response to a future pandemic, it was necessary to clarify the agency's statutory authority and its ability to access emergency relief funds. Here the report pointed to details of existing plans and statutes that needed revision. For instance, it noted that while the *Biological Incident Annex* designated HHS as the lead agency – with FEMA in support – existing policies and authorities did not provide the "necessary mechanisms" for the department to serve as lead. Thus, a 2016 Presidential Directive on "Enhancing Domestic Incident Management" did not include an administrative mechanism that would enable HHS to assign missions or provide funds to another agency during the response to a biological incident. Similarly, while the Public Health Service Act stated that HHS would lead the federal public health and medical response, it provided only limited authorities for HHS to facilitate this coordination. And while the 1976 National Emergencies Act authorized the president to declare a "national emergency" in response to a pandemic, it did not provide HHS with additional authorities to lead the emergency response. Moreover, the after-action report noted that while an emergency declaration under the 1988 Stafford Act was the best mechanism for releasing federal disaster relief funds, there was no precedent for a pandemic leading to such a declaration. The report thus recommended the codification of policies and procedures for HHS to lead, direct, and source funding in response to all public health emergencies.

The after-action report then turned from recommendations for statutory reform to the need to clarify existing plans, arguing that the *Biological Incident Annex* and the *Pandemic Crisis Action Plan* did not sufficiently detail the organization of government response to a pandemic emergency. For one thing, the plans did not spell out precisely what it would mean for HHS to serve as federal lead agency – that is, whether HHS would be the sole agency in charge or just the lead for public health and medical aspects, with FEMA in charge of overall "consequence management." Moreover, according to the report, exercise participants were unclear about the respective roles of various units within HHS such as ASPR and the Centers for Disease Control. Participants also reported confusion about the responsibilities of other federal agencies, which was attributed to lack of practice in implementing the "coordination mechanisms necessary to manage an influenza pandemic response." As the report explained, pandemics were "less often exercised" than more common disasters such as hurricanes, earthquakes, or wildfires. Here the report recommended that federal agencies update their pandemic plans to detail roles and responsibilities and to then "socialize these plans through trainings and exercises."

Another problem area revealed by the Crimson Contagion exercise concerned practices of communication and information sharing during an emergency response. For instance, it turned out that HHS and FEMA had incompatible IT systems. In addition, there were problems in developing a standard template for information sharing among federal, state, and local officials. Other communication-related problems revealed by the exercise concerned lines of authority: participants from state agencies were unsure to which federal agency they should send requests for information. Lines of authority for reporting within the federal government also needed to be clarified: both HHS and FEMA submitted "senior leader" briefings to the National Security Council. Finally, participants from state agencies were uncertain as to how they would receive information from CDC about results from nationally aggregated data as well as updates on the agency's public health guidance.

For our purposes here, a key lesson we can take from the after-action report is its narrow purview: the exercise as well as the post hoc assessment focused mainly on very specific details of administrative responsibility. From these documents, one can glean ASPR's priorities for the revision of plans and statutes as of 2019.[28] More generally, one can say that a given scenario-based exercise is designed within a particular planning horizon: it tests what its organizers have already diagnosed as problematic areas, and what is within the agency's purview in making recommendations for reform. Insofar as the Crimson Contagion exercise exposed problems that were not within ASPR's purview to address, the agency demurred from making recommendations. For instance, its after-action report noted that exercise participants expressed confusion about how decisions about school closures should be made, and, relatedly, that they voiced concern over the potential "cascading effects" of school closures. Here the report did not make any recommendations but suggested only that future exercises might "also include examination of the political aspects involved in managing pandemics." In retrospect, of course, we can say that such "political aspects" were among the most salient problems in the US response to Covid-19. Here, for example, we might point to conflicts that arose over the legitimacy of authorities' mandates on vaccines and masks; or to tensions around interruptions of social and economic life, such as school and business closures; or to deeper, more structural flaws exposed by the pandemic, such as long under-resourced local public health agencies without the capacity to track and manage outbreaks. These issues – which were beyond the purview of ASPR's mission – were not within the rubric of the test exercise.

Taking into consideration the various biological preparedness exercises that were conducted in the decades preceding the coronavirus pandemic, another key design feature becomes apparent: the organizers of a given exercise must select the characteristics of the pathogen that will be featured in its scenario. In turn, resulting recommendations will focus on mitigating vulnerabilities to this pathogen. For instance, the decision to feature a smallpox attack in the 2001 Dark Winter exercise led to a recommendation to acquire millions of doses of smallpox vaccine for storage in the Strategic National Stockpile. Similarly, the scenarios for most of the pandemic exercises in the years preceding Covid-19 featured an avian influenza virus. This selection, in turn, meant that certain virological and epidemiological factors that were critical in the response to Covid-19 were not incorporated into plans and exercises: for instance, the possibility that asymptomatic transmission would make containment especially difficult; or that the unavailability of biomedical countermeasures for at least a year would raise difficult questions about how long to impose social distancing measures; or that the elderly would be far more vulnerable to severe consequences than the young.

Even if the scenario of a future event persuades policymakers to undertake preparedness measures, whether those measures will prove worthwhile when an actual event occurs remains uncertain insofar as their efficacy may be specific to a particular scenario.

Responsibility for the future

We can now return to the question posed at the outset of the chapter: what kind of responsibility for the future does a scenario-based exercise generate? To what extent can we determine sites of blame for a current failure by demonstrating that "warnings went unheeded" after prior exercises? We moderns, as Luhmann argues, experience the future in terms of the risk of deciding. Unlike a world shaped by fate or divine will, the future for us is contingent upon decisions we make today. And in the aftermath of human-caused disaster – such as a plane crash, a nuclear accident, or a massive oil spill – we typically investigate what actions should have been taken to prevent the event's occurrence: what safety checks were not performed, what trainings were not conducted, what regulations were not enacted? Even in the case of what might have once been called an "act of God" – such as a Category 5 hurricane striking a city below sea level – we inquire into inadequacies of levee construction or the failure of the government agencies charged with response. The extension of the field of emergency management over the past 75 years – from the prospect of nuclear war to natural disasters to environmental catastrophes and pandemics – can be seen from this perspective. While the onset of a catastrophic event may not have been preventable, its consequences could have been mitigated through vulnerability reduction and preparedness measures.

In developing preparedness plans, one of the key techniques that emergency managers have devised for understanding vulnerability is the scenario-based exercise. However, the potential of an exercise to lead to measures that mitigate the consequences of an actual future event may turn out to be limited, both by the imagination of its designers and by the administrative bounds of its organizing agencies. We should not take for granted that such exercises (and their accompanying after-action reports) are best understood as warnings about an approaching future event that may be either heeded or ignored by decision makers. Rather, they should be seen as elements in an iterative planning process that seeks to clarify the structure of responsibility for an event that cannot be handled according to normal organizational structures. The aim of the exercise in this context is relatively circumscribed: it is designed not to foresee the future but to prioritize a set of administrative goals that have already been articulated by the agency that is its sponsor.

5

Emergency Use

In the summer of 2020, the long-simmering crisis in the authority of expert knowledge in the United States seemed to reach a boiling point. The rapid and deadly spread of the novel coronavirus in the previous months coincided with a bitterly fought presidential campaign. In its response to the pandemic, the Trump administration had thrown into question the very premise that the claims of technical experts should – or even could – be considered independently of political calculations. Respected government health institutions, such as the Centers for Disease Control and the National Institutes of Health, were sidelined from the management of the crisis, their experts' recommendations ignored or overruled. Experts based in federal regulatory agencies – part of what the president derisively called the "deep state" – were seen by the administration as inherently suspect. Urgent health-policy questions remained unsettled and even became sources of public protest: Should masks be required in public places? How should epidemiological thresholds for the closure of schools and businesses be determined? Should doctors be allowed to prescribe highly touted but unproven medications?

Regulatory science, as embodied in the technical guidelines and protocols issued by agencies such as the CDC and the Food and Drug Administration (FDA), had become a central object of political contestation. It was in this fraught context that the question of how soon a vaccine to contain the pandemic would be made available came into public view. As the date of the 2020 presidential election neared, President Trump staked his claim that his administration had adequately responded to the pandemic on the premise that the federal government's vaccine development program – Operation Warp Speed – would deliver a technical fix by the fall. Indeed, it seemed possible that the outcome of the election would hinge on the timing of what was ostensibly a technical decision: the regulatory authorization of a novel Covid vaccine. A simultaneously technical and political struggle ensued. The administration sought to draw on a relatively obscure administrative mechanism – the Emergency Use Authorization (EUA) – to accelerate the timeline for the evaluation of vaccine candidates. In turn, an alliance of academic experts, federal agency staff, and drug-industry leaders worked to forestall external interference into the regulatory process. What went unremarked during this high-stakes struggle was its historical condition of possibility: the establishment, a decade and a half earlier, of a space of regulatory flexibility in anticipation of a future biological emergency.

Rapid vaccine development

In April 2020, the Trump administration introduced Operation Warp Speed, an ambitious government-led effort to accelerate the development, production, and distribution of vaccines to address the pandemic emergency. Coordinated jointly by the Department of Health and Human Services (HHS) and the Department of Defense, the program contracted with several pharmaceutical and biotechnology companies to support research, development, and manufacturing for a Covid vaccine, with an initial US$10 billion budget. An agency within HHS, the Biomedical Advanced Research and Development Agency (BARDA), served as the financial interface between the federal government and the pharmaceutical industry. Given the prior history of vaccine development, the time frame envisioned by Operation Warp Speed was audacious: it sought to deliver 300 million doses of "safe and effective" Covid vaccines by early 2021.[1] A typical vaccine development process, including R&D, clinical trials, regulatory review, manufacturing, and distribution could take six years or more to complete, but Operation Warp Speed sought to reduce the timeline to roughly one year through a series of efficiency measures, including viral genome sequencing to identify vaccine candidates, large-scale clinical trials run in parallel with government-supported manufacturing, and an expedited regulatory evaluation procedure. By the summer of 2020, the program seemed to be on the verge of success: several vaccine candidates supported by Operation Warp Speed had already entered Phase III trials, each enrolling between 30,000 and 60,000 research subjects.

Accelerating the procedure for regulatory review was a critical element of the "warp-speed" strategy. Under normal circumstances, a vaccine candidate must go through a lengthy Biologics License Application (BLA) process before the FDA will approve it for entrance onto the market. The lengthy BLA review process involves a benefit–risk analysis conducted by FDA scientists – and in some cases by an external committee of experts as well – based on comprehensive evaluation of clinical-trial data provided by the vaccine developer. This technical procedure provides regulators with a form of what historian of science Theodore Porter describes as "mechanical objectivity." Through the use of such standardized, typically quantified techniques, Porter argues, vulnerable government agencies are able to defend themselves against accusations of idiosyncratic judgment or bias.[2] From the perspective of government regulators, adherence to such standard protocols ensures public confidence in the integrity of the agency's decisions.

However, in the context of the rapid spread of a novel infectious disease for which no effective vaccines or drugs were available, Operation Warp Speed planners anticipated the need for an alternative to the standard regulatory process. An EUA allows for the temporary use of an unapproved medical product if the Secretary of Health and Human Services has declared a "public health emergency" under section 564 of the Food, Drug, and Cosmetic Act. According to the law, the FDA may issue an EUA for a medical product if the available evidence indicates that it is "reasonable to believe" that the product in question "may be effective" in treating the condition identified by the emergency declaration. In other words, the standard, often lengthy procedure of the Biologics License Application can be attenuated. The EUA device thus provides the federal government with a flexible method for the rapid authorization of an unapproved medicine in the urgent and uncertain circumstances of a public health emergency. However, the very flexibility of the EUA process opens it up to the danger of the perception of external influence: by attenuating the lengthy technical process used to generate mechanical objectivity, the issuance of an EUA may be seen to compromise the integrity of a regulatory decision.

In contrast to the use of benefit-risk analysis to evaluate a potential new treatment for an already prevalent condition (such as heart disease, cancer, or diabetes), the EUA device is designed for an outbreak of a novel disease for which there are no existing approved treatments. The device was first introduced in the context of US bioterrorism-preparedness initiatives in the late 1990s and early 2000s. Biosecurity authorities had assembled the Strategic National Stockpile in order to prepare for a chemical, biological, radiological, or nuclear attack. The stockpile contained large troves of medical countermeasures such as smallpox and anthrax vaccines, nerve-gas antidote, and botulism antitoxin, many of which did not have FDA approval for their projected uses – and, indeed, could not be ethically tested on humans since the diseases in question were not present in the population. This became apparent as a problem in the immediate aftermath of the anthrax letter attacks of October 2001, when the lack of prior regulatory approval made it difficult to provide post-exposure anthrax vaccine to postal workers. National security officials worried about a scenario – such as a smallpox or anthrax attack – in which there would be an urgent need for mass treatment but not enough time for a prospective drug or vaccine to go through the regulatory approval process.

Congress addressed this apparent gap in preparedness as part of the 2004 Project Bioshield Act, which aimed to provide the government "with the ability to develop, acquire, stockpile and make available the medical countermeasures needed to protect the US population against weapons of mass destruction."[3] The Project BioShield legislation included a provision – the EUA – that amended the Food, Drug and Cosmetic Act to expedite the use of a potentially lifesaving countermeasure in the event of a mass-casualty attack.[4] Upon the declaration of a "public health emergency affecting national security," EUA authority allows the FDA to "facilitate availability and unapproved uses of [medical countermeasures] needed to prepare for and respond to CBRN emergencies."[5] The EUA mechanism was used for the first time in 2005 by the Department of Defense to enable the military to immunize soldiers against anthrax using a vaccine that had not received FDA approval.

In 2006, new legislation enacted in response to the threat of an avian influenza pandemic extended the framework of biological preparedness beyond the scenario of a bioweapons attack. The Pandemic and All-Hazards Preparedness Act expanded the scope of the EUA mechanism to include "emerging diseases such as pandemic influenza." The legislation provided the FDA with a list of criteria for evaluating an EUA application: the disease must be life threatening; it must be "reasonable to believe the product may be effective" for the specified use; the known and unknown benefits of the medicine must outweigh its known and potential risks; and there must be no available alternative. The EUA mechanism built in flexibility to allow for the exigencies of an as yet unknown future situation: in contrast to the standard procedures of a normal Biological License Application, in the case of an application for emergency use, the FDA would decide on a case-by-case basis what kinds of evidence concerning safety and efficacy would be necessary, and how the estimated benefit of a potential treatment would be weighed against its potential risk. For instance, an emergency vaccine that would be given to millions of healthy individuals would presumably have to reach a different threshold of safety in a benefit–risk analysis than would a potentially lifesaving drug intended for infected patients.

The EUA mechanism is distinct from the normal procedures of drug regulation in that it is part of the framework of "emergency government" as it took shape in the mid-twentieth-century United States.[6] American emergency government, developed in the contexts of World War II mobilization and Cold War nuclear preparedness, involves the use of anticipatory techniques that enable officials to manage a future crisis without recourse to extralegal measures. This form of government is oriented to the possibility of an unprecedented event – one that cannot be adequately managed through existing statutes and procedures. It seeks to provide the executive branch with devices that will enable rapid and flexible response to future emergencies whose precise characteristics cannot be predicted. In this sense, the official declaration of an "emergency" does not put government on an extralegal footing but rather is a distinct framework within normal governance. Through such measures, as legal scholar Kim Lane Scheppele has argued, emergencies have been “absorbed and rationalized within the system of public law rather than outside normal governance.”[7]

Underpinning the legislation that established the EUA procedure was the scenario of a future event, such as a biological attack or a pandemic, in which an alternative to the standard drug regulation process would be needed. In the case of such an event, according to Project BioShield, the FDA’s statutory requirement for a comprehensive review of clinical trial data could be suspended to enable a flexible response to the demands of a rapidly unfolding situation. The EUA device thus established a space of regulatory ambiguity: it would be up for negotiation and contestation how an authorization for emergency use might be granted. In the case of the authorization of a Covid-19 vaccine, an unintended consequence of this interpretive leeway was to open up the regulatory process to what some observers considered dangerous external pressure.

The Covid-19 emergency

On February 4, 2020, two weeks after the initial detection of the novel coronavirus in the United States, HHS Secretary Alex Azar officially declared the event a “public health emergency that has a significant potential to affect national security” under the Food, Drug, and Cosmetic Act, as amended by Project BioShield. Based on this declaration, the secretary then determined that “circumstances exist justifying the authorization” of medical devices not yet approved by the FDA – specifically, in vitro diagnostics for detecting the coronavirus.[8] Over the next several months, the FDA issued emergency authorizations for the temporary use of medical products to address Covid-19, including diagnostic tests, protective equipment, and medicines. The issuance of an EUA in late April 2020 to allow physicians to prescribe hydroxychloroquine for the treatment of Covid-19 proved controversial. The drug's efficacy was still under investigation at the time, but it had been promoted as a wonder drug by public figures, including the president. After several studies failed to demonstrate its efficacy – and, indeed, indicated potential harm – FDA withdrew its authorization for emergency use in mid-June.

The EUA procedure again sparked controversy in late August, when FDA Commissioner Stephen Hahn appeared at a press conference alongside President Trump and Secretary Azar to tout the success of convalescent plasma therapy in treating severe cases of Covid-19, announcing that his agency had issued an emergency authorization for its clinical use. Soon after the announcement, a number of scientists outside of government sharply criticized the commissioner for making exaggerated claims about the efficacy of the treatment, pointing to the results of published clinical trials which were significantly less robust than Hahn had suggested. Further, critics denounced Commissioner Hahn for being in thrall to an administration that was by this time widely seen as hostile to the scientific community. As Eric Topol, editor-in-chief of *Medscape Medical News*, wrote in an open letter to Hahn: "We cannot entrust the health of 330 million Americans to a person who is subservient to President Trump's whims, unprecedented promotion of unproven therapies, outrageous lies, and political motivations."[9]

Even more troubling to many observers was the possibility that the Trump administration would use the EUA device to prematurely authorize the use of a Covid-19 vaccine. Indeed, this was a more or less explicit strategy of the Trump campaign, which hoped that a rapid vaccine rollout would aid its reelection effort. As the *New York Times* reported in early August, "Trump campaign advisors privately call a pre-election vaccine 'the holy grail.'"[10] Here it should be recalled that during this period, the summer of 2020, the successful development of a Covid vaccine was generally considered to be the critical solution to the pandemic emergency – the only thing that could enable a return to normalcy. The scenario of an "October surprise vaccine" that would influence the election became more plausible in September with the confident announcement by the CEO of Pfizer that a "conclusive readout" of clinical trial results for its candidate vaccine would be available within the following month, after which the company would immediately request that the FDA issue an authorization for emergency use.[11] The president, meanwhile, claimed that "we're very close to that vaccine," indeed, "We think we can start sometime in October."[12]

In this context, a series of authoritative experts made public statements questioning the integrity of the EUA process. The editor-in-chief of *Science* magazine published a scathing editorial, assailing the Trump administration's health agencies for bowing to political pressure and calling on physicians to refuse to administer any vaccine authorized under questionable circumstances. "We now know that Redfield, Azar, and Hahn are not capable of, or willing to, stand up to President Trump," he wrote. "The medical community must stop this dance as we get closer to rolling out a vaccine for Covid-19 because we now know that we will not get any help from the federal government." Topol, in his open letter, called on Commissioner Hahn to pledge to conduct a rigorous vaccine assessment process or to immediately resign. He argued that public confidence in vaccines must be shored up by demonstrating the autonomy of the regulatory process from political influence – an assertion that would be repeated by multiple commentators over the next several weeks. "Any shortcuts will not only jeopardize the vaccine programs," he wrote, addressing Hahn, "but betray the public trust, which is already fragile about vaccines, and has been made more so by your lack of autonomy from the Trump administration and overt politicization of the FDA."[13]

A similar argument came from inside the government, as a group of senior FDA officials argued that the credibility of the agency's regulatory decisions depended on its insulation from external interference. "When it comes to decisions to authorize or approve the products we regulate," wrote the group in a *USA Today* op-ed, "we and our career staff do the best by public health when we are the decision makers."[14] The stakes, for public health, of preserving expert autonomy were high, the officials warned: "If the agency's credibility is lost because of real or perceived interference, people will not rely on the agency's safety warnings." Biotech and pharmaceutical industry leaders joined the chorus of opposition to political meddling in regulatory decisions. In an "open letter to the biopharmaceutical industry" members of the Biotechnology Innovation Organization (BIO) wrote that the "FDA should maintain its historic independence as the gold-standard international regulatory body, free from external influence." Again, the need to preserve public trust served as the rationale for a defense of technocratic authority: "This will assure the public that the FDA review process will adhere to the highest standards of scientific and political integrity."[15]

Thus, an alliance had formed among academic scientists, government regulators, and drug industry leaders to protect the vaccine authorization process from the perception of political interference. The assumption was that the success of a vaccination program would hinge not only on the therapeutic efficacy of the vaccine as demonstrated in clinical trials, but also on public confidence in the integrity of the regulatory process. Here the specter of vaccine hesitancy loomed: if a significant proportion of the population refused to take the vaccine – especially since there was uncertainty about the degree of therapeutic efficacy that an eventual vaccine would demonstrate – a mass vaccination program might well fail to stem the pandemic. A Covid vaccine was "unlikely to achieve herd immunity unless it has a high rate of effectiveness (> 50%) and wide public acceptance (> 70%)," as one health policy analyst argued. "Perceptions of political interference in regulatory approval generate distrust, while amplifying fears about a future vaccine's safety and effectiveness."[16] Of course, the campaign against political interference into the regulatory process, insofar as it involved a coalition of actors with a shared concern to protect the FDA's autonomy, was itself a political intervention.

Measuring public trust

In parallel to – and in interaction with – experts' defense of regulatory autonomy, multiple surveys reported diminishing public confidence in the regulatory process alongside decreasing willingness to take a prospective Covid vaccine. Between May and September 2020, according to a study by the Pew Research Center, the number of survey respondents who said they would either "definitely" or "probably" take an available vaccine declined from 72 percent to 51 percent, and over three-quarters of respondents indicated a belief that a vaccine would likely be approved before its safety and efficacy had been comprehensively assessed.[17] A CNN poll reported a drop from 66 percent to 51 percent from May to October in the percentage of those surveyed who said they would try to get a Covid vaccine once it was available. Similarly, Gallup reported a 16 percent decline from July to late September in the number of respondents who would be "willing to be vaccinated" if "an FDA-approved vaccine was available right now at no cost." Writing in the *Washington Post*, a group of former FDA commissioners cited the finding of an Axios-Ipsos poll that "42 percent of Americans lacked trust in FDA decision-making." The implications of these survey data were "potentially dire," the group argued, for addressing the day's "most urgent" question: "When the FDA approves a Covid-19 vaccine, will Americans accept it?"[18]

Following insights from the social studies of expertise, we should be cautious in interpreting the significance of these measures of public trust in a Covid vaccine. Public trust in regulatory science, as sociologist Gil Eyal notes, is not best understood as "an attitude measured by surveys," but rather should be seen as a by-product of institutional mechanisms embedded in social arrangements. Members of the public do not necessarily have a stable level of trust in agencies such as the FDA or CDC, Eyal argues, but rather what he calls a "vigilant trust," ready to be suspended or reinstated based on recent encounters or news. Trust can easily swing into distrust and then back again. It "is a moving target shifting with the winds," he writes, "sensitive to recent events or to how a question is formulated."[19] In this case, political winds were a likely source of the shifting public response to survey questions about the public's trust in a Covid vaccine. Although the Republican Party would later be associated with vaccine skepticism, in the late summer 2020 it was Democratic politicians who voiced suspicion of a possible Covid vaccine, insofar as its approval might be rushed by the Trump administration. "Let me be clear," said Joe Biden. "I trust vaccines. I trust scientists. But I don't trust Donald Trump, and at this moment, the American people can't either."[20] In the context of a polarizing election campaign in which one's position with respect to the administration's management of vaccine development could well depend on one's political self-identity, survey responses did not necessary indicate what a given member of the public was likely to actually do when faced with the concrete situation of an available, FDA-authorized vaccine.

For our purposes here, however, the question is not so much whether these surveys accurately measured a coherent entity – public trust – or how to explain the apparent decline in levels of trust in a potential Covid vaccine. Rather, what is of interest is how such measures of declining public trust were marshaled as a resource by scientists and regulatory officials who sought to insulate the FDA from external political pressure. Under these circumstances, the prospect of vaccine hesitancy changed its normative valence. For over two decades, scientists and public health specialists have considered vaccine hesitancy to be a problem demonstrating the need for improved "public understanding of science" – that is, as a problem of irrational fear sparked by rumor and misinformation, a deficit requiring correction. The task for experts and officials, in turn, has been to use the tools of "risk communication" – such as transparency, openness, and engagement – to assuage irrational public fear. But in late summer and early fall 2020, as the pandemic emergency intensified and the election approached, the relation of scientific authority to public distrust shifted: evidence of public distrust in a potential vaccine signaled the danger posed by political interference in expert judgment. From the perspective of those defending FDA autonomy, public distrust was a rational response to the Trump administration's efforts to undermine the technocratic authority of government regulators.

Defending regulatory autonomy

In September 2020, two pharmaceutical companies with promising vaccine candidates – Moderna and Pfizer – indicated that preliminary results from their clinical trials might be available as early as the following month. Each company had already manufactured millions of vaccine doses in anticipation of rapid authorization for distribution. To prepare their applications for an EUA, the companies requested guidance from the FDA on what data it would need in order to make a decision on granting an EUA for a novel vaccine candidate. Meanwhile, a bureaucratic struggle was brewing between FDA career scientists, on the one hand, and White House officials, on the other, over how regulators would evaluate Covid vaccine candidates as the results of vaccine developers' Phase III trials came in. FDA commissioner Hahn, stung by criticism of the EUA process from respected scientists, insisted that the agency would use stringent criteria for authorization and would subject all vaccine candidates to assessment by an external body of experts. "Decisions to authorize or approve" a vaccine, he testified before a Senate committee, "will be made by the dedicated career staff at FDA through our thorough review processes, and science will guide our decisions."[21]

FDA staff drew up a set of proposed guidelines requiring vaccine manufacturers to "provide adequate information to assess a vaccine's benefit–risk profile" in their application for an EUA.[22] In a public statement, the FDA's lead vaccine evaluator emphasized that "increasing trust in vaccines" was the rationale for these new requirements.[23] "[B]eing transparent about the data that we will evaluate in support of the safety and effectiveness of these vaccines," he wrote, "is critical to build trust and confidence in their use by the public." The new guidelines for an EUA sought to emulate, within a circumscribed time frame, the kind of regulatory scrutiny that a normal biologics license application (BLA), based on the FDA's rigorous evaluation of comprehensive clinical trial data, would require. The effort was to at least partially reconstruct the mechanical objectivity of a standard benefit–risk analysis as a means to publicly demonstrate the agency's integrity.

Two of the proposed guidelines were of particular note in relation to the question of the timing of an EUA: First, clinical trial subjects would have to be tracked for at least two months for potential adverse reactions. And second, a minimum number of severe Covid cases would have to be included in the control group numbers. It was not lost on White House officials that the adoption of these guidelines would extend the timeline for a potential authorization of a novel vaccine beyond the date of the election. In response, the *Washington Post* reported on September 25, the White House demanded that the FDA provide "very detailed justification" for the extended timeline required by the proposed guidelines.[24] According to President

Trump, the proposed regulatory requirements were "a political move more than anything else."[25] And the president's chief of staff complained about "new guidance that came out just a few weeks before we're hopefully going to have some very good results on three clinical trials from some of these vaccines." By early October, reported the *New York Times*, White House officials were "blocking strict new federal guidelines for the emergency release of a coronavirus vaccine, objecting to a provision that would almost certainly guarantee that no vaccine could be authorized before the election on November 3." The approval of the FDA staff's proposed guidelines was "now seen as highly unlikely."[26]

At this moment of intensifying struggle between the White House and the FDA, various external authorities weighed in to support the FDA's autonomy in determining procedures for evaluating an EUA application, invoking the need to secure public trust in regulatory authority. "If the White House takes the unprecedented step of trying to tip the scales on how safety and benefits will be judged," as the group of former FDA commissioners argued, "the impact on public trust will render an effective vaccine much less so."[27] In an open letter to HHS Secretary Azar, the president of the Biotechnology Innovation Organization insisted that "new FDA guidance should be finalized and communicated with those on the frontlines developing potential vaccines." The guidance must also "be shared more broadly with the American public," she continued, alluding to the fragility of public trust in regulatory science. "We cannot allow a lack of transparency to undermine confidence in the vaccine development process."[28]

At this point, with a high stakes meeting of the agency's external advisory committee on vaccines scheduled to meet in October to discuss the review process, FDA staff performed what the editor of *Science* later called "bureaucratic jujitsu." They stealthily inserted the new guidelines into briefing materials that the agency posted online for participants in advance of the advisory committee meeting.[29] As the date of the meeting approached – perhaps due to the collective pressure of the FDA scientists' allies in academia, government, and the private sector – the White House did not, in the end, block the proposed guidelines. With the new guidelines in place, it would be impossible for any of the most advanced vaccine candidates to receive an EUA before the election. FDA scientists celebrated the clearance of the new guidelines, reported the *New York Times*, which described the event as "a win for career civil servants."[30] Meanwhile, President Trump dismissed the outcome as "another political hit job," making it "more difficult for them to speed up vaccines for approval before Election Day."[31]

Conclusion

The public health emergency of the Covid-19 pandemic generated an experiment in the provisional reconstruction of a regulatory process designed to ensure the perceived objectivity of governmental expertise. The construct of public trust and the specter of vaccine hesitancy, wielded by an alliance of academic scientists, industry leaders, and government regulators, enabled the FDA to fend off external interference and – from the perspective of experts and officials – sustain the perceived integrity of the vaccine authorization process. What occasioned this struggle was the distinctive bureaucratic space in which the evaluation of Covid vaccine candidates took place. In response to the pandemic emergency, the federal government had established a state of regulatory exception, in which the EUA was a tool that made it possible to curtail the normal lengthy drug-approval process. As a preparedness device, the EUA had been put in place over a decade and a half earlier with a specific scenario in mind, in which there would be no time to perform a normal regulatory evaluation of the safety and efficacy of a novel medical countermeasure to address a public health emergency. The structure of a future emergency situation had been envisioned in advance; what had not been envisioned was the potential for abuse of the EUA procedure. The EUA opened up the possibility for external political influence to shape an ad hoc regulatory decision. In this context, US regulatory officials sought to preserve their autonomy – at a moment of intense political pressure – by invoking the need to preserve public trust as a way to ensure the efficacy of a mass vaccination campaign.

While this alliance was effective in staving off an "October vaccine surprise" by the Trump administration, it did not, in the end, manage to de-politicize the question of vaccine safety and efficacy. With the arrival of the authorized vaccines as well as a new presidential administration in early 2021, public distrust of the regulatory process reappeared. But now the political valence of distrust had shifted: as part of its repudiation of the "deep state," right-wing commentators and politicians now fostered skepticism of the FDA's authorization of what they claimed was an "experimental" vaccine. The task for authorities, in turn, was – once again – to try to reassure those in doubt that there was no objective basis for distrust in regulatory expertise.

6

Gain of Function

In the weeks following the initial appearance of the virus causing Covid-19, authorities in the field of zoonotic disease sought to provide an explanatory framework that would make sense of the virus's sudden emergence and rapid spread. Writing in the *New York Times* in late January 2020, journalist David Quammen noted that experts had long anticipated an epidemic caused by the transmission of an animal virus to humans. Quammen had been warning about the danger to humans posed by zoonotic diseases since his 2012 bestseller, *Spillover: Animal Infections and the Next Human Pandemic*. It was "utterly unsurprising to scientists who study these things," he wrote, that the virus causing Covid-19 had "emerged from a nonhuman animal, probably a bat."[1] The appearance of Covid-19 was just one incident within a longer trajectory of viral emergence: the current outbreak was "part of a sequence of related contingencies that stretches back into the past and will stretch forward into the future." Quammen then turned to the explanation for this long-running sequence. The circumstances leading to this pattern included "a perilous trade in wildlife for food," billions of hungry humans, "some of them impoverished and desperate for protein," and the fact that people could now "travel every which way by airplane." Thus, ecological disturbances resulting from human exploitation of natural resources were leading to "increasing viral exchanges," exemplified by the novel coronavirus.

The ongoing transmission of emerging viruses from animals to humans was an epidemiological story for Quammen, but it also carried moral significance in that it led us to understand our own responsibility for the situation in which we found ourselves. The appearance of Covid-19 should not be seen as "a novel event or a misfortune that befell us," he explained, but rather as "part of a pattern of choices that we humans are making." Fortunately, there was a way to combat this "sequence of related contingencies": through investment in scientific research on emerging viruses. Pointing to cutting-edge research in the field of viral ecology, Quammen wrote that "brilliant, dedicated scientists" were going "into bat caves, swamps, and high-security containment laboratories" to "bring out bat feces and blood" so that key questions about these emerging pathogens could be answered. Perhaps, through such research, the inexorable process of zoonotic spillover could be interrupted.

The following month, one of the scientists to whom Quammen paid tribute, disease ecologist Peter Daszak, elaborated on this explanatory framework. In an essay in the *New York Times* entitled "We Knew Disease X was Coming. It's Here Now," Daszak recalled that two years earlier, at a meeting of the World Health Organization, he had been among a "group of experts" that had predicted how "the next pandemic" would begin.[2] The group had anticipated that the next pandemic would "likely result from a virus originating in animals and would emerge somewhere on the planet where economic development drives people and wildlife together." Daszak's argument in the essay focused not on the immediate response to Covid-19 but rather on what he called "the really big picture"

– that is, the future: "Pandemics are on the rise, and we need to contain the process that drives them."

Daszak argued that this rise in pandemics was being driven by zoonotic disease emergence that resulted from human disturbance of the natural environment: "spillovers are increasing exponentially as our ecological footprint brings us closer to wildlife in remote areas and the wildlife trade brings these animals into urban centers." The emergence of zoonotic disease was, as Quammen had suggested, not only a story about viruses but was also a narrative about the damage wrought by advanced industrial civilization: intensive "road-building, deforestation, land clearing and agricultural development, as well as globalized travel and trade, make us supremely susceptible to pathogens like coronaviruses." Given the inevitable emergence of novel pathogens under these circumstances, our goal should be to discover and sequence unknown viruses before they spread widely – to "know your enemy." Here Daszak had a proposed solution: he would lead a "Global Virome Project" that, at an estimated cost of US$100 million per year over ten years, would venture into the wilderness to gather and store a vast compendium of the world's animal viruses in order to assess which of these had the potential to spread to humans and become pandemics.

This was a busy period for Daszak. In parallel with this pitch for a major investment in virus gathering based on the premise of the zoonotic emergence of Covid-19, he also sought to counter a competing hypothesis concerning the pandemic's origin: that it had been the result of a laboratory accident at the Wuhan Institute of Virology, a well-known site of experimentation on bat coronaviruses located in the city where the initial outbreak had taken place. The week before his "Disease X" essay appeared, Daszak organized a group of "public health scientists" to co-author a letter to the *Lancet* expressing "solidarity with all scientists and health professionals in China who continue to save lives and protect global health during the challenge of the COVID-19 outbreak." Citing published analyses of the genome of SARS-CoV-2 that "overwhelmingly conclude this coronavirus originated in wildlife," the authors wrote, "We stand together to strongly condemn conspiracy theories suggesting that COVID-19 does not have a natural origin."[3] In the months and years to come, the letter's assertion that any alternative to the zoonotic emergence hypothesis was a conspiracy theory would have a chilling effect on efforts to explore the question of Covid's origin.

Further support for the claim of a natural zoonotic origin soon came from a group of leading virologists in a paper published in *Nature Medicine* in March 2020, entitled "The Proximal Origin of SARS-CoV-2." Like the *Lancet* letter organized by Daszak, the "proximal origin" paper sought to allay any concerns that the virus might have been the result of a laboratory accident at the Wuhan Institute of Virology. While acknowledging that it was not yet possible to definitively prove or disprove any theory of the virus's origin, the authors wrote that, given what was known about its features, "we do not believe that any type of laboratory-based scenario is plausible."[4] Rather, "zoonotic transfer" was the most likely explanation for the emergence of the virus. However, the authors noted, more research on potential animal sources would be needed to confirm the hypothesis: "obtaining related viral sequences from animal sources would be the most definitive way of revealing viral origins."

In May, the World Health Organization charged an international team of researchers with expertise in virology and disease ecology, including Daszak, to travel to China to investigate Covid-19's origins. Along the lines suggested by the *Nature Medicine* letter, the WHO resolution establishing the research team's mission cited the need "to identify the zoonotic source of the virus and the route of introduction to the human population" – that is, to find the animal origin of the virus. After a series of delays, the WHO investigative team arrived in Wuhan in January 2021, with the country still in lockdown, and conducted interviews with Chinese scientists and public health specialists, but it was not given access to any raw data. The team's report, issued in March 2021, announced that its findings supported the zoonotic spillover hypothesis: the report assessed that it was "likely to very likely" that the virus had been introduced to humans through an intermediate animal host, most likely at the Huanan Seafood Market, a center for the wildlife trade. Meanwhile, the report dismissed the competing scenario of a laboratory release as the origin of the virus as "extremely unlikely."[5]

Post hoc assessment

In parallel to its investigation of the origins of Covid-19, the WHO set into motion the process of assessing the global response to the pandemic. This process of assessment typically involves the appointment of a commission of experts whose task is to draw lessons from the event and point to the need to anticipate similar future crises. Thus, for example, after the 2009 H1N1 pandemic, a review committee charged to evaluate the WHO response reported that the organization had difficulty adjusting to unexpected characteristics of the disease. Noting that the H1N1 virus had proven less severe than initially anticipated, the committee warned that the future would bring deadlier outbreaks of novel pathogens, and that "the world is ill-prepared for a severe pandemic or for any similarly global, sustained and threatening public health emergency."[6] Five years later, after the catastrophic Ebola epidemic in West Africa, another WHO review committee warned that "the world cannot afford another period of inaction until the next health crisis."[7] Such assessments, in turn, seek to galvanize resources and structure organizational reform in order to ward off future catastrophe. In accordance with this structure, in the fall of 2020 WHO Director-General Tedros established an Independent Panel for Pandemic Preparedness and Response "to review experience gained and lessons learned" from the international health response to the coronavirus pandemic.[8] The task of the Independent Panel was both to assess the sources of failure in the global response and to "make recommendations to improve capacity for global pandemic prevention, preparedness, and response." The panel's official report, released in May 2021, echoed prior such assessments: "the world was not prepared and had ignored warnings which resulted in massive failure," the panel found. Having slept through such prior warnings, it urged, the "world needs to wake up" so that it may adequately "prepare for the future."[9]

The future to be prepared for was one in which evermore infectious disease emergencies could be expected. Here the panel's report drew on the explanatory framework of zoonotic emergence. "Population growth and accompanying environmental stresses are driving an increase in emerging novel pathogens," it explained. Moreover, through air travel these emerging pathogens could reach any place in the world "in a matter of hours." The Covid-19 pandemic had been sparked by "just such a virus of zoonotic origin whose emergence was highly likely," the report continued. A corollary to this assumption of the increasing incidence of zoonotic disease emergence was the need to build systems to monitor the future onset of such pathogens, alert officials, and quickly move to contain any outbreaks. As the Independent Panel's report put it, "zoonotic outbreaks are becoming more frequent, increasing the urgency for better detection and more robust preparedness." Among its suite of recommendations were to "invest in preparedness now" and to "establish a new international system for surveillance, validation, and alert" – perhaps, one might add, along the lines of Daszak's proposed Global Virome Project. The framework of zoonotic emergence thus not only explained the origin of Covid-19; it also structured the lessons learned by global health authorities as they sought to guide future action. Given the inevitable and ongoing emergence of new infectious diseases, as the panel argued, what was needed was more government investment in techniques of preparedness.

But even as the theory of zoonotic emergence as the source of the pandemic framed both retrospective assessments and recommendations for future reform, an unsettling counter-hypothesis gained sudden and unexpected currency among a different group of observers: the long-marginalized argument that the pandemic might have originated not with a spillover event in the wild but rather through the accidental release of an experimental virus from a laboratory. Up to this point, the suggestion of a lab accident as a plausible source of the pandemic was mostly ignored by science journalists who deferred to the authors of the "proximal origin" letter and their virology colleagues.

Heightened attention to this counterhypothesis was sparked by a series of events in the spring of 2021. First, the WHO investigative team's report on Covid's origin was met with widespread criticism among both global health officials and scientists. Upon receiving the report at the end of March, WHO Director-General Tedros expressed concern that the team's conclusions were not well founded. Pointing to difficulties that the team had encountered in accessing raw data held by the Chinese government, he announced that he expected "future collaborative studies to include more timely and comprehensive data sharing." Despite the team's confident pronouncement that the Huanan seafood market had been the site of the initial outbreak, Tedros argued that the "role of animal markets is still unclear," and that, given the team's limited ability to access raw data, "I do not believe this assessment was extensive enough." In relation to the scenario of a laboratory accident, he cautioned against foreclosing the possibility: "Although the team has concluded that a laboratory leak is the least likely hypothesis, this requires further investigation, potentially with additional missions involving specialists." More generally, Tedros pronounced, "as far as WHO is concerned all hypotheses remain on the table" insofar as "[w]e have not yet found the source of the virus." The WHO would continue the investigation insofar as the determination of past responsibility was an essential guide for preventive action in relation to a dangerous future: "we owe it to the world to find the source so we can collectively take steps to reduce the risk of this happening again."[10]

The WHO investigative team's findings were further challenged in May, when a group of eighteen prominent scientists published a letter in the journal *Science* calling for further research into Covid-19's origins. The scientists criticized the WHO team's report for its confidence in the hypothesis of zoonotic emergence despite a lack of evidence "in clear support of either a natural spillover or a lab accident."[11] The letter insisted on the need to take both hypotheses seriously "until we have sufficient data," and argued that any further investigation should be "transparent, objective, data-driven, inclusive of broad expertise, and responsibly managed to minimize the impact of conflicts of interest." This last point was a veiled reference to the controversial role of Daszek as a member of the WHO investigative team, given EcoHealth Alliance's longstanding collaboration with the Wuhan Institute of Virology in the investigation of bat coronaviruses and thus its possible implication in the scenario of a lab accident. Daszak meanwhile came under similar criticism for his role in organizing the *Lancet* letter, in which he did not declare a conflict of interest.

Further support for reopening the question of Covid's origins came from established science journalists such as Nicholas Wade and his former *New York Times* colleague William McNeil. After a lengthy survey of the available evidence, Wade argued in the *Bulletin of the Atomic Scientists* that while "no definitive conclusion can be reached," those who favor the lab leak theory "can explain all the available facts about SARS2 considerably more easily than can those who favor natural emergence."[12] McNeil, in turn, noted that while there had previously been a consensus around zoonotic emergence, "more and more scientists feel misled," and he had finally been convinced to "stop worrying and love the lab leak hypothesis."[13] Also at around this time, reports surfaced of US intelligence findings that several scientists at the Wuhan Institute of Virology had been hospitalized with Covid-like symptoms in November 2019, before the first officially reported cases of the disease.[14] Meanwhile, a year and a half into the pandemic, scientists had yet to identify an intermediary host animal that could confirm the natural spillover hypothesis, thus keeping open the question of the initial source of the outbreak.[15]

The situation could be characterized as one of diagnostic uncertainty – both about how to retrospectively attribute blame and about the horizon of future reform. For some commentators, the question of Covid's origins was a distraction from the real problems at hand: the need to contain the still unfolding pandemic and to better prepare for inevitable future ones. But there remained the question of how to think about the significance of the pandemic in relation to possible future reforms. How was it possible to prepare for "the next pandemic" if one did not know what had brought about the current one? Responsibility for an avoidable catastrophe pointed in different directions, depending upon one's assumption about the origin of the virus – either to authorities' lack of preparedness for the inevitable emergence of a dangerous new virus, or to scientists' irresponsible research that had inadvertently sparked a pandemic. And future reform efforts would, in turn, have different targets: either improving surveillance and response systems to prepare for emerging viruses, or regulating research to prevent future laboratory accidents.

As journalist David Wallace-Wells would later put it, there was no consensus on the origin of Covid but rather there were "different narratives imposed by different factions trying to make sense of the same uncertain picture."[16] This condition of what he called "epistemological limbo" was exacerbated by the fact that the origins debate was set within a highly polarized political environment. For those on the left, it was safest to view the lab leak hypothesis as a conspiracy theory promulgated by right-wing xenophobes; for those on the right, it seemed a damning indictment of the machinations of the deep state. As David Quammen eventually conceded, given the lack of definitive evidence on either side, his continued inclination in favor of the zoonotic spillover hypothesis was shaped by his own "prior beliefs."[17]

Viral traffic

Much of the public commentary on the potential implications of the lab leak hypothesis focused on what it would imply for culpability – whether of the Chinese government, the experimental virology community or US funding agencies.[18] But beyond this search for a proximate culprit, the hypothesis pointed to broader questions about the confluence of actors at the heart of the story: an environmental NGO based in New York devoted to collecting samples of viruses from wild animals around the world; a virology laboratory in Wuhan doing experimental research on bat coronaviruses; and the US National Institutes of Health, which supported a collaboration between those two entities as part of a larger portfolio of funding for basic research in the virology of emerging diseases. Here we must try to understand what principle of intelligibility guided researchers to take blood, saliva, and fecal samples from bats living in obscure caves in southern China, bring these samples to a laboratory in a faraway city, analyze viral fragments found in the samples, and experiment on them to explore their transmissibility among humans. How, in other words, did disease ecology meet experimental virology under the auspices of government research to improve public health? To address these questions, we must turn to the initial articulation of the framework of zoonotic emergence in the late 1980s, at the height of the HIV/AIDS crisis and toward the end of the Cold War, as a group of life scientists began to consider the future of infectious disease. It is here that we can find an initial articulation of the idea that monitoring animal viruses in the present might curtail human epidemics in the future.

In May 1989, an interdisciplinary conference on the topic of "emerging viruses" was held in Washington, DC.[19] The premise of the conference, co-sponsored by Rockefeller University and the National Institutes of Health, was that public health must take into account the centrality of human action in driving the emergence and spread of novel infectious diseases. Participants pointed to examples such as the evolution of new strains of influenza as a result of farming practices in Asia that intermingled ducks and pigs, the spread of dengue across oceans via water lingering in used tires, and the role of new techniques of maize production in extending the range of Argentine hemorrhagic fever.

One of the conference organizers, virologist Stephen Morse of Rockefeller University, proposed the concept of "viral traffic" to describe the movement of novel or already existing viruses to new species or new populations.[20] As Morse described it, the emergence of novel infectious diseases was a story about the unintended ecological consequences of modern industrial and agricultural development. Thus, for example, large dam projects in the developing world had led to the expansion of the range of mosquito-borne diseases such as Rift Valley fever. Industrialized meat production in the United Kingdom had fostered the appearance of mad cow disease. Large-scale rural-to-urban migration often introduced remote pathogens to larger populations, as in the case of the virus causing Lassa fever. Meanwhile, the advent of international air travel meant that an emerging virus could rapidly spread around the world, potentially sparking a pandemic.

The story of emerging diseases also pointed to the need for new forms of public health intervention. In order to address the threat posed by novel pathogens, Morse argued, we must become better viral "traffic engineers." An initial step would be to establish a global disease surveillance mechanism: a network of monitoring stations located in tropical areas and staffed by trained field epidemiologists could alert international health authorities to the emergence of a novel and deadly virus. This surveillance network should be attentive to "viral traffic signals," such as deforestation, dam construction, disruptive changes in agricultural practice, or major population migrations.

Such anticipatory knowledge might prevent the onset of future pandemics: "Most viruses that today are worldwide were once localized," Morse observed. AIDS, for instance, had begun as an emerging viral disease. If the right tools of detection and containment had been in place, it "could have been stopped at the pre-crisis stage." But the goal of pandemic prevention was not yet technically feasible – it would require the development of a "methodology for assessing the likelihood that a given animal virus will emerge as a human pathogen." Here he left open the question of how one might calculate the probability that a given animal virus would make the jump between species and become easily transmissible among humans.

In the meantime, according to Morse, the ongoing emergence and spread of novel pathogens into human populations was inevitable. Recent epidemics "should force the realization that new viruses will always be imminent" and that "tragedies like the AIDS epidemic will be repeated." As agricultural and industrial development caused further ecological disturbances, he predicted, "episodes of disease emergence are likely to become more frequent." To address this intensifying threat, government support for research into the processes through which new diseases emerged was urgently needed. With a better scientific understanding of viral evolution, he concluded, "we should be in a position to circumvent emerging diseases at fairly early stages." Over the next two decades, a research program at the intersection of disease ecology and experimental virology would coalesce around this goal.

Epidemic intelligence

Drawing on the assumptions of the "viral traffic" framework, international health authorities sought to implement a global surveillance system that could detect and rapidly contain novel pathogens. Epidemiologist Donald Henderson, who had led the WHO smallpox eradication campaign in the 1970s, provided an initial vision of a global system for detecting the onset of emerging diseases.[21] Henderson's vision built on the field of "epidemic intelligence," developed at the Center for Disease Control during the Cold War, which involved training field epidemiologists to track reports of outbreaks and quickly respond to contain them.[22]

Henderson proposed to extend the tools of epidemic intelligence – which had been designed to detect outbreaks of already known infectious diseases – to anticipate the emergence of novel ones. Such a system, he argued, would be of use not only for monitoring emerging diseases but also for the early detection of a bioterrorist attack. As director of the Johns Hopkins Center for Civilian Biodefense Strategies in the late 1990s, Henderson was well placed to make the case to policymakers for such an initiative. In the aftermath of the 2001 anthrax letters, this "dual use" approach to disease surveillance attracted increasing support from the US national security establishment, given the premise that early detection of a novel pathogen – whether naturally occurring or the result of a malevolent actor – would be critical to the possibility of containment.[23]

There were political as well as technical challenges to building a global system to detect emerging pathogens. National governments were often hesitant to report outbreaks to international authorities. At the outset of the 2003 SARS epidemic, the Chinese government refused to allow foreign experts into the country to investigate, underlining the need for a global system that would enable the rapid detection of and response to the outbreak of a novel infectious disease.[24] Soon after, the specter of an avian flu pandemic accelerated efforts to construct such a system, including the adoption of revised International Health Regulations that would enable the WHO to declare a "public health emergency of international concern" upon the initial detection of a novel pathogen. The goal was to push WHO member states to rapidly report any such outbreaks and to allow international health authorities to investigate them.[25]

Over the next several years, entrepreneurial scientists pitched tools for viral outbreak detection that could help achieve the goal of "stopping the next pandemic before it begins," as *Wired* magazine put it in a 2007 story on "the plague fighters."[26] Epidemiologist Larry Brilliant proposed to build a digital surveillance system that would trawl the internet and global news to detect signs of novel health threats.[27] Primatologist Nathan Wolfe promoted a method of "viral forecasting" that involved collecting samples of bushmeat from local markets across sub-Saharan Africa.[28] Zoologist Peter Daszak of EcoHealth Alliance conducted genetic analyses of virus samples taken from wildlife around the world with the aim of predicting the onset of emerging diseases, eventually securing millions of dollars in grants for virus gathering from NIH, USAID, and others.[29]

As the H5N1 virus continued to circulate globally in migratory birds, concern that the virus would mutate to become more easily transmissible among humans drove an intensification of basic research on viral emergence – research that was supported by national governments, multilateral agencies, and philanthropic NGOs. Viral ecologists argued that a pandemic strain would most likely emerge at the duck–pig interface in East Asia and then be carried around the world by migratory waterfowl, a scenario depicted by journalist Laurie Garrett in a 2005 *Foreign Affairs* essay entitled, "The Next Pandemic?"[30] To track potentially dangerous mutations of the H5N1 virus, molecular surveillance programs regularly conducted genetic analyses of virus samples taken from migratory birds and poultry populations.[31] But such surveillance efforts posed a familiar question: How could scientists know which viral strains to look for? What were the signs that an animal virus was becoming more easily transmissible among humans?

Here a new set of scientific actors entered the picture, in the context of growing investment from the National Institutes of Health (NIH) in research on the problem of viral emergence. A group of influenza virologists argued that it would be possible to simulate the natural process of viral evolution in the laboratory. The premise of their research was that experimentally pushing the H5N1 virus in the direction of human transmissibility would help molecular surveillance efforts by making it possible to identify genetic sequences linked to the ability to infect humans.[32]

The project of studying how avian influenza viruses might become more easily transmissible among mammals was taken up as part of the Department of Health and Human Service's (HHS) 2005 *Pandemic Influenza Plan*. In an appendix to the plan, the National Institutes of Health – located within HHS – pledged support for basic research in influenza virology, including projects to understand the "genetic changes that permit an influenza virus to suddenly acquire the ability to transmit between species."[33] This clause referred to an investigative method that would later become widely known as "gain-of-function" research, in which scientists experimentally manipulated viruses in order to study characteristics such as virulence and transmissibility. Between 2001 and 2007, annual federal funding for basic research in influenza virology, managed by the National Institute of Allergy and Infectious Diseases within NIH, jumped from US$15 million to US$212 million.[34] Much of this growth in funding for basic research on influenza hinged on the premise of a potential mutation, in the wild, of the H5N1 virus in the direction of increased human transmissibility.

Gain of function

When the H1N1 (swine flu) virus began to spread widely among humans in the spring of 2009, it seemed at first that it might be "the next pandemic" that health authorities had been warning about. But H1N1 turned out to have relatively mild effects on human populations, and WHO officials were eventually accused by critics of overreacting to the appearance of the new strain – of having pushed governments to invest huge sums in what turned out to be unnecessary mass vaccination campaigns.[35] By this time, meanwhile, the dire threat of an H5N1 avian influenza pandemic seemed to be waning. Perhaps – as some influenza virologists were beginning to suggest – the H5N1 virus was unlikely, after all, to mutate to become easily transmissible among humans.[36]

However, other virologists continued to make the case for the virus's viability as a pandemic threat – and therefore for the continued need to fund basic research on its transmissibility. In late 2011, when Dutch virologist Ron Fouchier announced at an international conference in Malta that his laboratory had created a strain of H5N1 that could be passed via aerosol transmission among ferrets (an animal model for human influenza infection), he explained the rationale for artificially creating what he described as "one of the most dangerous viruses you can make." While there were respected scientists who thought "that H5N1 could never become airborne between mammals," he said, "I wasn't convinced. To prove these guys wrong, we needed to make a virus that is transmissible."[37] In other words, to demonstrate the plausibility of a spillover event in the wild, he sought to create an easily transmissible strain of the virus in the lab.

Fouchier's announcement sparked an intense debate among life scientists and biosafety specialists over the risks and benefits of gain-of-function research on dangerous pathogens that played out over the next several years. According to advocates of the research, experimentally manipulating viruses to make them more virulent or transmissible would contribute to pandemic preparedness by enabling molecular surveillance efforts – such as sampling migratory birds for avian influenza – to recognize the emergence of dangerous pathogens in time to contain them. As NIH leaders Francis Collins and Anthony Fauci wrote in a December 2011 op-ed in defense of federal support for research like Fouchier's, "In defining the mutations required for mammalian transmission, public health officials are provided with genetic signatures that, like fingerprints, could help scientists more readily identify newly emergent, potentially harmful viruses, track their spread and detect threatening outbreaks."[38]

Critics of gain-of-function research on avian influenza, meanwhile, charged that the rationale for such research was tenuous at best. First, they argued, the research program took for granted a vast technical capacity for the molecular surveillance of potential animal hosts that was highly unrealistic given limited resources. As a *Nature* article on H5N1 surveillance noted, "In 2010, the world's poultry population was estimated at 21 billion, yet only around 1,000 flu sequences from 400 avian virus isolates were collected."[39] Second, the program assumed that viral strains developed in the laboratory through gain-of-function research would anticipate the strains that were likely to emerge in "nature." But, critics argued, there was no basis for such an assumption. As one scientist memorably put it, "Would nature have come up with the dachshund?"[40]

Critics of the research also argued that a significant recent record of laboratory accidents resulting in the release of dangerous viruses, along with a woefully insufficient regulatory apparatus, militated against government support for this type of gain-of-function research. Their major worry was that such research might spawn exactly what it was meant to prevent. As a group of scientists concerned with biosafety wrote in 2014, the lab-based creation of pathogens with pandemic potential "entails a unique risk that a laboratory accident could spark a pandemic killing millions."[41] For these critics, the hypothetical benefit of assessing the pandemic potential of emerging viruses did not outweigh the catastrophic risk of unleashing an actual pandemic. Thus, two scenarios confronted one another with no means of technical resolution: a naturally emerging virus, whose onset might be anticipated and even prevented through the results of viral transmission research, versus the accidental release of a pandemic virus as a result of this very research.

In this uncertain terrain, federal funding agencies struggled to find an agreed-upon method of technical risk assessment that could guide regulatory decisions.[42] Meanwhile, despite an official moratorium on federal support for gain-of-function research from 2014 to 2017, such experimentation, supported by the NIH, continued and extended to new areas.

The route to Wuhan

The two major strands of research on viral emergence – disease ecologists gathering samples from wildlife in the field and experimental virologists manipulating pathogens in the laboratory – converged in the investigation of bat coronaviruses found in caves in southern China. In June 2014, the NIH funded a proposal for research on "understanding the risk of bat coronavirus emergence," led by Peter Daszak in collaboration with the Wuhan Institute of Virology. The collaborative research program would address questions on "the origin, diversity, capacity to cause illness, and risk of spillover" of bat coronaviruses and involved "conducting laboratory experiments to analyze and predict which newly discovered viruses pose the greatest threat to human health."[43]

According to the proposal, the project would test such "emergence potential" – described as the potential for the "interspecies transmission" of novel coronaviruses – "using reverse genetics, pseudovirus and receptor binding assays, and virus infection experiments across a range of cell cultures from different species and humanized mice." Thus, the project sought to address the question that Stephen Morse had posed over two decades earlier in his essay on "regulating viral traffic": how to assess "the likelihood that a given animal virus will emerge as a pathogen." The way to address this question, for Daszak and his collaborators in Wuhan, was first to collect bat coronaviruses from caves in southern China, and then to manipulate these viruses in the laboratory to see whether they might become more easily transmissible among mammals.[44]

A decade after the initiation of the collaboration between EcoHealth Alliance and the Wuhan Institute of Virology, there were two ways to understand the retrospective significance of this research program – as either the prescient forecast or the dangerous progenitor of the Covid-19 pandemic. In this sense, we can understand our ongoing situation of diagnostic uncertainty as a question of which route of viral traffic to follow: zoonotic spillover, as exemplified by the movement of SARS in the early 2000s from bats to civet cats to humans via the trade in wildlife; or a new potential route, from the bat caves of southern China to a virology laboratory in Wuhan, as part of a cosmopolitan project in the life sciences – initially proposed in 1989 – to investigate the pandemic potential of emerging viruses. As Quamman's January 2020 essay had put it, "we made the coronavirus." But it was not clear whether it was ecological disruption or laboratory experimentation that was at fault. The stakes of this determination were high, not only for determining the sites of failure that had led to the present catastrophe, but also in targeting interventions designed to forestall "the next one."

Epilogue

On May 11, 2023, the Department of Health and Human Services announced the end of the public health emergency for Covid-19. Well before this official endpoint, officials and experts had begun a process of evaluating governmental failures and proposing future reforms. The early results of this assessment process could be glimpsed in the public hearings and official reports produced by the US Congress. In April 2021, the Senate Committee on Homeland Security and Governmental Affairs held a hearing on "the federal government's preparation for, and response to, the coronavirus pandemic."[1] The hearing was devoted to the problem of accountability and critical rectification in response to what was already widely understood to be a catastrophic failure in the nation's response to the pandemic. In his introduction to the session, the committee chair, Sen. Gary Peters of Michigan, laid out the hearing's agenda: "We have to examine and confront our failures, identify and build on what went right, and propose reforms to ensure our nation can combat this pandemic, and be better prepared to prevent and respond to future pandemics," he pronounced. The federal government had been developing and testing pandemic plans since 2005, he noted, prompting the question of why the United States nonetheless had suffered from among the highest rates of Covid-19 incidence in the world. "More than 562,000 Americans have now lost their lives," he said. "Tragically, it didn't have to be this way." The hearing would investigate where blame for the tragedy lay.

The committee solicited testimony on sources of the failed pandemic response from a series of experts from the worlds of emergency management and public health. These witnesses pointed to a litany of technical and institutional failures, from the CDC's faulty early testing to the fragility of the medical supply chain to confusion over leadership of the federal response. One of the hearing's witnesses touched on a theme that extended beyond the narrow, technical diagnoses that were offered by most of these experts, the question of "imagination." Senator Peters asked Julie Gerberding, the former director of the Centers for Disease Control, about the early stages of the pandemic – the weeks from late February to early March 2020 – a period during which the number of cases in the United States "increased 1,000-fold." What steps should the federal government have taken at that point to mitigate the rapid spread of the disease? Gerberding responded as an epidemiologist, reflecting on what had blinded experts to the fact that something novel was occurring, and that a more proactive response was needed. In retrospect, she said, health authorities should have understood "early in the course of things that asymptomatic transmission was happening" at a rate "unprecedented in disease transmission." They should have been able to see that the disease was not being contained, that it was spreading widely. Instead, most authorities assumed that, like other coronaviruses, the virus causing Covid-19 could only be spread by people experiencing symptoms of the disease.

Reflecting on this critical early period, Gerberding pointed out that sampling studies could have been done that would have accelerated scientific knowledge about the transmission rate "so that we would be better able to predict where to go look for cases even when testing wasn't widely available." And here she suggested a diagnosis of the source of the epidemiological failure: "So, in a sense, this was a failure of imagination, a failure to appreciate that this wasn't going to be like SARS or MERS, where the efficiency of transmission from person to person was low. This was a disease that would spread like wildfire, and we responded as if it were sort of business as usual." Existing pandemic plans had not envisioned a quickly spreading coronavirus; these plans had focused on influenza, which was known to spread rapidly. The past, in other words, weighed heavily on health authorities' interpretation of their present: when a novel coronavirus appeared, it was unimaginable – at the outset – that its key characteristics would be radically unlike previous coronavirus outbreaks.

While the focus of Gerberding's response was on a lack of epidemiological imagination, on infectious disease experts' assumption at the early stages of the coronavirus outbreak that it was "business as usual," her comments point us toward a broader range of questions. Insofar as we can consider governmental preparedness to hinge on the development of techniques of the imagination, we can ask: to what extent were preparedness experts able to imagine the unprecedented? How had pandemic preparedness sought to incorporate the possibility of an uncertain future in its planning efforts? In other words, what forms of imagination were built into US pandemic preparedness planning? And did that which was difficult or impossible to imagine prove significant in contributing to its "failure"? As we saw in chapter 1, the United States was ostensibly the leading country in the world in its level of pandemic preparedness, at least as measured by a 2019 assessment. And yet, as one of the senators noted, one year into the pandemic, with just 4 percent of the global population, the country had suffered 25 percent of global cases. How can we understand this apparent disjuncture between the future of infectious disease outbreaks that preparedness experts anticipated and the actual present that arrived in early 2020?

In his opening remarks at the Senate hearing, the committee's ranking member, Sen. Rob Portman of Ohio, suggested that the key question to be asked about the government's failed response to the pandemic was "Why were we unprepared?" As this book has suggested, the senator may have been asking the wrong question, given the nation's investment, over the prior decades, in techniques of preparedness that were implemented soon after the onset of the pandemic. Rather, a better question might have been, "What was preparedness unable to anticipate?" As we have seen, health officials and emergency managers implemented many long-standing preparedness measures at the outset of the pandemic, and these measures had impressive accomplishments: for instance, closing down much of social life while keeping basic economic activities functioning, efficiently setting up emergency medical facilities in urban areas, and stimulating the rapid development of novel vaccine candidates. In this regard, the existing preparedness apparatus might be seen as a kind of success. Nonetheless, these measures proved, in many cases, to have unanticipated effects – or to have been designed to address different problems than the ones that were actually posed by the SARS-CoV-2 virus.

Thus, it is not that global health security indicators were incorrect in their assessments, but that they emphasized capacities that did not prove especially salient for managing the pandemic that occurred. They were a solution, as it turned out, to a different problem than the one posed by Covid-19. Essential worker policy was impressively successful in what it set out to achieve: to reduce the spread of the disease through social interaction while enabling the critical functions underpinning collective life to continue. But, focused on this specific task, it did not anticipate the controversies that would arise upon its implementation – whether around the side effects of school closures, the thresholds of disease incidence that would be used to guide reopening, or the social inequities involved in the ongoing exposure of essential workers to the risk of infection. The Strategic National Stockpile was certainly well prepared, holding millions of doses of vaccines and drugs, but it was prepared for a different portfolio of risks than those presented by the coronavirus, given the threat assessments that guided decisions about stockpile provision. In the years leading up to the pandemic, numerous scenario-based exercises tested plans and identified gaps in public health preparedness, but their capacity to mitigate potential vulnerabilities was constrained by the organizational task for which they were designed. The Emergency Use Authorization was successful in its aim to guide novel treatments rapidly through the clinical development process but did not foresee that a flexible mode of authorization might open up the regulatory process to perceptions of external influence and undermine public trust in the resulting vaccine. Finally, federal funding of gain-of-function research as a means of building a system of viral surveillance did not envision that this research might pose the risk of sparking – rather than preventing – a pandemic caused by a novel pathogen.

It would not be accurate, then, to say that the United States was "unprepared" for the onset of a novel and deadly virus; indeed, the various techniques of preparedness developed over the decades before Covid-19, if measured according to the criteria they set for themselves, were often effective. But, when put into practice as part of the response to the coronavirus pandemic, they in many cases failed to address the key problems posed by the virus or generated unanticipated side effects. To understand these unexpected effects, as I hope the prior chapters have shown, we must examine the context in which they were initially developed, and the problems that were most salient to the experts who designed them. As for whether such an understanding is useful in preparing for "the next one," to address this question requires us to ask at the same time what kind of "next one" we should anticipate. And this, it would seem, is a question that preparedness is ill-equipped to answer.

Notes

Introduction

1 White House, "Remarks by President Trump, Vice President Pence, and Members of the Coronavirus Task Force in Press Conference." February 26, 2020. Accessed at: https://trumpwhitehouse.archives.gov/briefings-statements/remarks-president-trump-vice-president-pence-members-coronavirus-task-force-press-conference/

2 Several excellent books have already appeared on the response to the pandemic in the United States during the first year. For a journalistic analysis, see Lawrence Wright, *The Plague Year: America in the Time of Covid* (Knopf, 2021); the perspective of a former public health official is provided by Scott Gottlieb in *Uncontrolled Spread: Why Covid-19 Crushed Us and How We Can Defeat the Next Pandemic* (Harper, 2021); for an engrossing sociological account of the pandemic as it was experienced in New York City, see Eric Klinenberg, *2020: One City, Seven People, and the Year Everything Changed* (Knopf, 2024).

3 For the history of the idea of an epidemic curve, see David S. Jones and Stefan Helmreich, "The Shape of Epidemics," *Boston Review*, June 26, 2020.

4 Howard Markel et al., "Nonpharmaceutical Influenza Mitigation Strategies, US Communities, 1918–1920 Pandemic," *Emerging Infectious Diseases* 12(12) (December 2006).

5 Centers for Disease Control (2007), "Interim Pre-pandemic Planning Guidance: Community Strategy for Pandemic Influenza Mitigation in the United States." Accessed at: https://www.cdc.gov/flu/pandemic-resources/pdf/community_mitigation-sm.pdf

6 Howard Markel, "America's Coronavirus Endurance Test," *New Yorker*, August 6, 2020.

7 This context is elaborated in greater detail in Stephen J. Collier and Andrew Lakoff, *The Government of Emergency: Vital Systems, Expertise, and the Politics of Security* (Princeton University Press, 2021).

8 For a detailed discussion of the process of revising the International Health Regulations, see Alexandre White, *Epidemic Orientalism: Race, Capital, and the Governance of Infectious Disease* (Stanford University Press, 2023), ch. 4.

9 *The World Health Report 2007: A Safer Future. Global Public Health Security in the 21st Century* (Geneva: World Health Organization, 2007).

10 The story of how techniques of preparedness that were invented during the Cold War were applied to the novel threat posed by infectious disease beginning at the end of the twentieth century is told in my book, *Unprepared: Global Health in a Time of Emergency* (University of California Press, 2017).

11 Cited in Colin Koopman, *Genealogy as Critique: Foucault and the Problems of Modernity* (Indiana University Press, 2013), p. 85.

12 For a lucid discussion of the debates over the authority of regulatory knowledge about risk, see Gil Eyal, *The Crisis of Expertise* (Polity, 2019).

13 Center for Health Security and Nuclear Threat Initiative, *Global Health Security Index* (2019), p. 5. Accessed at: https://www.ghsindex.org/wp-content/uploads/2019/10/2019-Global-Health-Security-Index.pdf

Chapter 1 Preparedness Indicators

1 Center for Health Security and Nuclear Threat Initiative, *Global Health Security Index* (2019), p. 5. Accessed at: https://www.ghsindex.org/wp-content/uploads/2019/10/2019-Global-Health-Security-Index.pdf

2 The White House, "Remarks by President Trump, Vice President Pence, and Members of the Coronavirus Task Force in Press Conference," February 26, 2020. Accessed at: https://trumpwhitehouse.archives.gov/briefings-statements/remarks-president-trump-vice-president-pence-members-coronavirus-task-force-press-conference/. A comparative study of national responses to the pandemic pointed to the puzzle of "why some nations have contained the virus completely while others have struggled to prevent multiple waves of community transmission," noting that "despite impressive US achievements in biomedicine, and despite extensive planning for pandemic preparedness, the US record in addressing the public health crisis of Covid-19 is among the worst in the world." Sheila Jasanoff, Stephen Hilgartner, J. Benjamin Hurlbut, Onur Özgöde, and Margarita Rayzberg (2021), *Comparative Covid Response: Crisis, Knowledge, Politics*. Harvard Kennedy School. Accessed at: https://www.futuresforumonpreparedness.org/research

3 Mattias Kaiser, Andrew Tzer-Yeu Chen, and Peter Gluckman, "Should Policy Makers Trust Composite Indices? A Commentary on the Pitfalls of Inappropriate Indices for Policy Formation." *Health Research Policy and Systems* 19(40) (2021). As anthropologist Manjari Mahajan noted, "It is striking how little correlation there is between countries' preparedness rankings on the GHS Index and the actual experiences with COVID-19." Mahajan, "Casualties of Preparedness: The Global Health Security Index and Covid-19," *International Journal of Law in Context* 17(2) (2021).

4 "Editorial: The US Was Supposed to be Equipped to Handle a Pandemic. So What Went Wrong?" *Washington Post*, December 26, 2020.

5 Nicholas Kristof, "America and the Virus: A Colossal Failure of Leadership," *New York Times*, October 22, 2020.

6 Branko Milanovic, "Beware of Mashup Indexes: How Epidemic Predictors Got It All Wrong." Accessed at: https://glineq.blogspot.com/2021/01/. Ezra Klein, "The Covid Policy That Really Mattered Wasn't a Policy," *New York Times*, February 6, 2022. Manjari Mahajan (op. cit) develops this argument in more detail, pointing out that the key factors determining a country's success in responding to the pandemic were very different from those emphasized by the index. Such characteristics as state capacity, quality of leadership, coordinating different levels of government, and public health infrastructure at the community level proved more critical than the specific technical capacities measured by the GHSI.

7 Sheila Jasanoff, "'Preparedness' Won't Stop the Next Pandemic," *Boston Review*, December 8, 2021.

8 Robert Tucker Omberg and Alex Tabarrok, "Is it Possible to Prepare for a Pandemic?" *Oxford Review of Economic Policy* 38(4) (2022): 853.

9 Michael Lewis, *The Premonition, A Pandemic Story* (W. W. Norton, 2021), pp. xx–xiii.

10 The Covid Crisis Group, *Lessons from the Covid War: An Investigative Report* (PublicAffairs, 2023), p. 12.

11 Joshua Lederberg, "Medical Science, Infectious Disease, and the Unity of Humankind," *Journal of the American Medical Association* 260(5) (August 5, 1988). See also Alexandre White, *Epidemic Orientalism: Race, Capital, and the Governance of Infectious Disease* (Stanford University Press, 2023), p. 180.

12 For an analysis of the "emerging diseases worldview," see Nicholas King, "Security, Disease, Commerce: Ideologies of Postcolonial Global Health," *Social Studies of Science* 32 (2002).

13 Laurie Garrett, *The Coming Plague: Newly Emerging Diseases in a World Out of Balance* (Farrar, Straus and Giroux, 1994); Richard Preston, *The Hot Zone: The Terrifying True Story of the Origins of the Ebola Virus* (Anchor, 1995).

14 For the longer history of this way of understanding disease emergence, see Warwick Anderson, "Natural Histories of Infectious Disease: Ecological Vision in Twentieth-Century Biomedical Science," *Osiris* 19(1) (2004).

15 Stephen S. Morse, "Regulating Viral Traffic," *Issues in Science and Technology* 7(1) (1990).

16 David P. Fidler, "From International Sanitary Regulations to Global Health Security: The New International Health Regulations." *Chinese Journal of International Law* 325 (2005). The discussion of the IHR revision process in this chapter draws on Lakoff, *Unprepared* (2017).

17 David L. Heymann and Guénaël Rodier, "Global Surveillance, National Surveillance, and SARS," *Emerging Infectious Diseases* 10(2) (2004).

18 World Health Organization, *International Health Regulations (2005)*, 2nd edn (Geneva: World Health Organization, 2008).

19 World Health Organization, *A Safer Future* (2007), p. 11.

20 In the meantime, the WHO Department of Global Capacities, Alert and Response developed a "monitoring framework" to track member states' progress toward meeting the requirement. The monitoring framework defined the eight capacities that were "needed for detecting and responding to the specified human hazards and events" – including surveillance, response, preparedness, and risk communication. To measure each country's progress toward meeting the core capacity requirement, the monitoring framework included twenty-eight different indicators "relevant to advancing the objective of developing capacity to detect, assess, report, notify, verify and respond to public health risks and emergencies of national and international concern." World Health Organization: IHR Core Capacity Monitoring Framework, "Checklist and Indicators for Monitoring Progress in the Development of IHR Core Capacities" (2013), p. 14. Accessed at: https://www.who.int/publications/i/item/who-hse-gcr-2013-2

21 Jennifer B. Nuzzo and Matthew P. Shearer, "International

Engagement is Critical to Fighting Epidemics," *Health Security* 15(1) (2017).

22 Tom Frieden, "Why Global Health Security is Imperative", *The Atlantic*, February 14, 2014.

23 United Nations, *Protecting Humanity from Future Health Crises: Report of the UN High-Level Panel on the Global Response to Health Crises* (United Nations, 2016). Accessed at: https://www.un.org/en/our-work/global-health-crises-task-force

24 World Health Organization, "Implementation of the International Health Regulations (2005): Report of the Review Committee on the Role of the International Health Regulations (2005) in the Ebola Outbreak and Response." Report by the Director-General, May 13, 2016. Accessed at: https://apps.who.int/gb/ebwha/pdf_files/WHA69/A69_21-en.pdf

25 "Editorial: First Response, Revisited," *Nature* 514 (September 25, 2014): 459.

26 World Health Organization (2016), p. 51.

27 The White House, "Executive Order: Advancing the Global Health Security Agenda to Achieve a World Safe and Secure from Infectious Disease Threats" (November 4, 2016). Accessed at: https://obamawhitehouse.archives.gov/the-press-office/2016/11/04/executive-order-advancing-global-health-security-agenda-achieve-world#:~:text=No%20single%20nation%20can%20be,partner%20countries'%20measurable%20capabilities%20to

28 Ibid. Nuzzo and Shearer (2017) later wrote: "US leadership through the GHSA has breathed new life into the IHR, drawing much-needed awareness from national governments and providing a multilateral mechanism to provide support to low-resource nations."

29 Theodore M. Porter, "The Flight of the Indicator," in Richard Rottenberg, Sally E. Merry, Sung-Joon Park, and Johanna Mugler, *The World of Indicators: The Making of Governmental Knowledge Through Quantification* (Cambridge University Press, 2015), p. 34.

30 World Health Organization, *Joint External Evaluation Tool: International Health Regulations (2005)* (Geneva: World Health Organization, 2nd edn, 2018). Accessed at: https://www.who.int/publications/i/item/9789241550222

31 Richard Rottenberg and Sally Engle Merry, "A World of Indicators: The Making of Governmental Knowledge through Quantification," in Rottenberg et al., *The World of Indicators* (2015).

32 United Nations Development Program, *Human Development Index*. Accessed at: http://hdr.undp.org/en/content/human-development-index-hdi.

33 The World Bank, *World Development Indicators*. Accessed at: https://datatopics.worldbank.org/world-development-indicators/.

34 United Nations Sustainable Development Goals, *SDG Indicators*. Accessed at: https://unstats.un.org/sdgs/indicators/indicators-list/.

35 WHO, *Joint External Evaluation Tool* (2016), p. 5.

36 Nuzzo and Shearer, "International Engagement" (2017), p. 34.

37 As Nuzzo and Shearer put it, "The GHSA provides support for nations to assess their existing health security capacities, identify gaps, and formulate plans to fully implement the IHR to ensure domestic and international capacity to detect, prevent, and respond to health security threats." Nuzzo and Shearer, "International Engagement" (2017), p. 34.

38 Wilmot James, "Op-ed: In an age of Zika and a Threat of Biochemical Terror, Health Security Must Be Everybody's Concern." *Daily Maverick*, April 2, 2017. It might be noted that – however useful these programs have been – in most cases it would be difficult to demonstrate their specific relevance for addressing Covid-19.

39 For instance, legal scholar Lawrence O. Gostin argued: "The countries most affected by Ebola . . . rank lowest in global development, lacking essential public health infrastructure." Gostin,

"Ebola: Towards an International Health Systems Fund," *The Lancet* 384 (9951) (October 11, 2014), p. e49.

40 Center for Health Security and Nuclear Threat Initiative, *Global Health Security Index* (2019), p. 5.

41 As two scholars of global governance have noted, the Joint External Evaluation (JEE) tool was not as useful as the GHSI for making cross-country comparisons because scores were not available in the form of an accessible cross-national dataset; rather, JEE emphasized the qualitative nature of the analysis and making concrete policy recommendations. Alexander E. Kentikelenis and Leonard Seabrook, "Governing and Measuring Health Security: The Global Push for Pandemic Preparedness Indicators," *Global Policy* 13(4) (2022).

42 Beth Cameron bio at the Nuclear Threat Initiative, accessed at: https://www.nti.org/about/people/beth-cameron/

43 Center for Health Security and Nuclear Threat Initiative, *Global Health Security Index* (2019), p. 31.

Chapter 2 Essential Workers

1 Editorial Board, "'You're on Your Own,' Essential Workers Are Being Told," *New York Times*, April 20, 2020. In late October, Vice President Mike Pence claimed the mantle of "essential worker" in order to continue campaigning after several of his staff members were diagnosed with Covid-19. Marilynn Marchione, "Health Experts Question Pence Campaigning as Essential Work," *Associated Press*, October 25, 2020.

2 Adie Tomer and Joseph W. Kane, "How to Protect Essential Workers during COVID-19," Brookings Institution Report. March 31, 2020. Accessed at: https://www.brookings.edu/articles/how-to-protect-essential-workers-during-covid-19/

3 Christopher C. Krebs, "Memorandum on Identification of Essential Critical Infrastructure Workers during COVID-19 Response," US Department of Homeland Security, Office of Cybersecurity and Infrastructure Security, March 19, 2020.

4 Ben Christopher, "Who is 'Essential' Now that Californians have to Stay at Home?" *CalMatters*, March 20, 2020; Mihir Zaveri, "The WWE is Now Considered an 'Essential Service' in Florida," *New York Times*, April 14, 2020.

5 Ari Natter, "'Essential' Label Stirs Business Frenzy to Make Trump's List," *Bloomberg News*, April 14, 2020; Valerie Strauss, "The Trump Administration Declared Teachers 'Essential Workers.' Here's What that Means," *Washington Post*, August 21, 2020.

6 Editorial Board, "'You're On Your Own,' Essential Workers Are Being Told."

7 Shawn Hubler, Thomas Fuller, Anjali Singvia, and Juliette Love, "Many Latinos Couldn't Stay Home. Now Virus Cases are Soaring in Their Communities," *New York Times*, June 26, 2020.

8 Department of Health and Human Services (March 13, 2020), *PanCAP Adapted US Government Covid-19 Response Plan*, Annex C: Operations, pp. 22–3.

9 Siobhan Roberts, "Flattening the Coronavirus Curve," *New York Times*, March 27, 2020.

10 Dr. L. Nedda Dastmalchi and Dr. Healther J. Kagan, "Flattening the Coronavirus Curve: It's Happening but It's Not Over Yet." ABC News, April 15, 2020.

11 Kerry Crowley, "Governor Newsom: COVID-19 Cases Have Quadrupled, Hospitalizations Have Tripled in Last Six Days," *San Jose Mercury News*, April 1, 2020.

12 "Andrew Cuomo New York Coronavirus Briefing, April 1" (2020). Accessed at: https://www.rev.com/blog/transcripts/andrew-cuomo-new-york-coronavirus-briefing-transcript-april-1

13 The coronavirus guidelines were based on measures sketched out in HHS's adapted Pandemic Crisis Action Plan. HHS, *PanCAP Adapted US Government Covid-19 Response Plan*, 2020.

14 "The President's Coronavirus Guidelines for America: Thirty Days to Slow the Spread." Accessed at: https://trumpwhitehouse

.archives.gov/wp-content/uploads/2020/03/03.16.20_coronavirus-guidance_8.5x11_315PM.pdf

15 Cybersecurity and Infrastructure Security Agency, "Guidance on the Essential Critical Infrastructure Workforce: Ensuring Community and National Resilience in COVID-19 Response," March 19, 2020. Accessed at: https://www.cisa.gov/resources-tools/resources/guidance-essential-critical-infrastructure-workforce

16 Executive Department, State of California, Executive Order N-33-20, March 19, 2020. Accessed at: https://covid19.ca.gov/img/Executive-Order-N-33-20.pdf

17 Ana Swanson and David Yaffe-Bellany, "Trump Declares Meat Supply 'Critical,' Aiming to Reopen Plants," *New York Times*, April 29, 2020.

18 The quotation is from James T. Lowe, "The Theory of Strategic Vulnerability," cited in Stephen J. Collier and Andrew Lakoff, *The Government of Emergency: Vital Systems, Expertise, and the Politics of Security* (Princeton University Press, 2021).

19 William Sherman, *Air Warfare* (New York, 1926), cited in Stephen J. Collier and Andrew Lakoff, "Vital Systems Security: Reflexive Biopolitics and the Government of Emergency," *Theory, Culture and Society* 32(2) (2015): 19–51, 27.

20 Barry M. Katz, *Foreign Intelligence: Research and Analysis in the Office of Strategic Services*, 1942–1945 (Cambridge, MA: Harvard University Press, 1989).

21 Peter Galison points to the mirroring process through which civil defense experts applied the lessons of World War II strategic bombing to US urban planning. "War Against the Center," *Grey Room* 4 (Summer 2001): 5–33.

22 See Collier and Lakoff, *The Government of Emergency*.

23 These resource categories were replicated – with the addition of health, water, and government operations – in the 1964 *National Plan for Emergency Preparedness*. A more recent version can be found in the Federal Emergency Management Administration's *National Response Framework* (2021). Accessed at: https://www.

fema.gov/emergency-managers/national-preparedness/frameworks/response .

24 For a discussion of the use of civil defense resources for other forms of disaster planning during the Cold War, see Scott Gabriel Knowles, *The Disaster Experts: Mastering Risk in Modern America* (Philadelphia: University of Pennsylvania Press, 2013). For the migration of these techniques to the problem of emerging infectious disease, see Andrew Lakoff, *Unprepared: Global Health in a Time of Emergency* (University of California Press, 2017).

25 These agencies included the Office of Defense Mobilization of the 1950s, the Office of Emergency Preparedness in the early 1960s, and the Federal Emergency Management Agency, established in 1979.

26 This and the below quotations are from: President's Commission on Infrastructure Protection, *Critical Foundations: Protecting America's Infrastructures: A Report of the President's Commission on Critical Infrastructure Protection* (October 1997). Accessed at: https://sgp.fas.org/library/pccip.pdf. On the emergence of the field of critical infrastructure protection, see Stephen J. Collier and Andrew Lakoff, "The Vulnerability of Vital Systems: How 'Critical Infrastructure' Became a Security Problem," in Myriam Anna Dunn and Kristian Soby Kristenson (eds), *Securing the "Homeland": Critical Infrastructure, Risk, and (In)Security* (Routledge, 2008).

27 Department of Homeland Security, *National Infrastructure Protection Plan (NIPP) 2013: Partnering for Critical Infrastructure Security and Resilience*, 2013, p. 1. Accessed at: https://www.cisa.gov/resources-tools/resources/nipp-2013-partnering-critical-infrastructure-security-and-resilience

28 Homeland Security Council, *National Strategy for Pandemic Influenza* (The White House, 2005). Accessed at: https://www.cdc.gov/flu/pandemic-resources/pdf/pandemic-influenza-strategy-2005.pdf

29 As a federal interagency emergency response plan, the National Response Framework can be seen as a descendant

of Mobilization Plan D-Minus. Department of Homeland Security, *Biological Incident Annex to the Response and Recovery Federal Interagency Operational Plans*, 2017. Accessed at: https://www.govinfo.gov/content/pkg/GOVPUB-HS-PURL-gpo134285/pdf/GOVPUB-HS-PURL-gpo134285.pdf

30 Stephanie Lie and Rong-Gong Lin II, "California Fails to Protect Latino Workers as Coronavirus Ravages Communities of Color," *Los Angeles Times*, July 15, 2020.

31 Jacey Fortin, "After Meat Workers Die of Covid-19, Families Fight for Compensation," *New York Times*, October 6, 2020.

Chapter 3 The Strategic National Stockpile

1 See, for instance, Andrew Jacobs, Matt Richtel, and Mike Baker, "'At War With No Ammo': Doctors Say Shortage of Protective Gear is Dire," *New York Times*, March 19, 2020; and Amy Goldstein, Lena H. Sun, and Beth Reinhard, "Desperate for Medical Equipment, States Encounter a Beleaguered National Stockpile," *Washington Post*, March 28, 2020.

2 Lena H. Sun, "Inside the Secret US Stockpile Meant to Save Us All in a Bioterror Attack," *Washington Post*, April 24, 2018.

3 Sarah Mervosh and Katie Rogers, "Governors Fight Back Against Coronavirus Chaos: 'It's Like Being on eBay with 50 Other States,'" *New York Times*, March 31, 2020.

4 Jacobs, Richtel, and Baker, "'At War With No Ammo.'"

5 Jacobs, Richtel, and Baker, "'At War With No Ammo.'"

6 Amy Brittain, Isaac Stanley-Becker, and Nick Miroff, "White House's Pandemic Relief Effort Project Airbridge is Swathed in Secrecy and Exaggerations," *Washington Post*, May 8, 2020.

7 Andrew Jacobs, "Grave Shortages of Protective Gear Flare Again as Covid Cases Surge," *New York Times*, July 8, 2020.

8 Olga Khazan, "Why We're Running out of Masks," *The Atlantic*, April 10, 2020.

9 US Congressional Research Service, "The Strategic National

Stockpile: Overview and Issues for Congress," Report 47400. Updated September 26, 2023. Accessed at: https://crsreports.congress.gov/product/pdf/R/R47400

10 Senate Committee on Homeland Security and Governmental Affairs. Full Committee Hearing: "The Role of the Strategic National Stockpile in Pandemic Response." June 24, 2020. Accessed at: https://www.hsgac.senate.gov/hearings/the-role-of-the-strategic-national-stockpile-in-pandemic-response/

11 This point was made at the hearing by several experts on the strategic national stockpile. As its former director, Greg Burel, noted, the stockpile's "original design and its current funding do not support responding to a nationwide pandemic of this severity."

12 For illuminating discussions of the practice of stockpiling in relation to broader security questions, see Andreas Folkers, "Freezing Time, Preparing for the Future: The Stockpile as a Temporal Matter of Security," in *Security Dialogue* 50(6) (2019); and Frédéric Keck, "Stockpiling as a Technique of Preparedness," in Joanna Radin and Emma Kowal (eds), *Cryopolitics: Frozen Life in a Melting World* (MIT Press, 2017).

13 The history of US stockpiling is elaborated in greater detail, in relation to the invention of the "science of flows", in Collier and Lakoff, *The Government of Emergency*. Folkers describes a parallel story in interwar Germany, in which government stockpiling was a "technique for securing the flow of materials that make both industrialized warfare and industrialized life possible." Folkers, "Freezing Time, Preparing for the Future."

14 The concepts of cushion and substitutability came from the work of WWII civilian economists who advised the allied air campaign on how to interrupt enemy production systems, developing what they called "the economics of strategic target selection." See Barry M. Katz, *Foreign Intelligence: Research and Analysis in the Office of Strategic Services*, 1942–1945 (Cambridge, MA: Harvard University Press, 1989).

15 Norvin C. Kiefer, "Role of Health Services in Civil Defense," *American Journal of Public Health and the Nation's Health* 40(12) (1950), p. 1489.

16 John M. Whitney, "The Federal Civil Defense Administration Medical Stockpile," *Military Medicine* 188(4) (April 1956): 260.

17 The medical stockpiling program had been transferred to the US Public Health Service in 1961 after a reorganization of emergency planning functions in the executive branch.

18 Price noted that "components of the hospitals have been used in several natural disasters," citing their use in Hurricane Beulah, which struck Texas in 1967, but emphasized that in such cases fully equipped hospitals were nearby and could take in patients after "initial treatment at the disaster site." Robert L. Price, "Use of the Packaged Disaster Hospital in Nigeria," *Public Health Reports* 85(8) (1970): 664.

19 Describing the use of the packaged hospital to treat a wide range of conditions in Port Harcourt, Price enthused: "The packaged disaster hospital performed magnificently as a general hospital and, if it is ever used to provide care for large numbers of casualties, it also has the capacity to relieve medical problems created by loss of other facilities, medications, food, services, and other features of a hostile environment." Price, "Use of the Packaged Disaster Hospital in Nigeria" (1970), p. 664.

20 Much of it was "unfit for use," the *New York Times* reported, and the rest "can be given to state agencies or sold to private bidders." Harold M. Schmieck, Jr., "US to Dispose of Huge Medical Supplies," *New York Times*, February 19, 1973.

21 The existence of these large stocks of bioweapons had been revealed to US biodefense officials by a recent defector from the Soviet Union who had been a leader of the secret Soviet bioweapons program. See Ken Alibek, *Biohazard: The Chilling True Story of the Largest Covert Biological Weapons Program in the World – Told from Inside by the Man Who Ran It* (Hutchinson, 1999).

22 Richard Preston, *The Cobra Event* (Random House, 1997).

23 Stephen J. Collier, Andrew Lakoff, and Paul Rabinow, "Biosecurity: Toward an Anthropology of the Contemporary," *Anthropology Today* 20(5) (2004).

24 As Andreas Folkers argues, stockpiles reduce uncertainty by establishing something to rely on in the face of an unknown future; this has a securing effect in the present even when the future that is anticipated never comes to fruition.

25 US Congressional Research Service, "The Strategic National Stockpile."

26 For a detailed discussion of the Dark Winter exercise, see Andrew Lakoff, *Unprepared: Global Health in a Time of Emergency* (University of California Press, 2017).

27 The Bush administration's Secretary of Health and Human Services, Tommy Thompson, took credit for this addition to the stockpile. Another federal program that was shaped by the findings of the Dark Winter exercise was the 2002 Smallpox Vaccination Program, which sought – unsuccessfully – to inoculate 300,000 first responders against smallpox. See Dale Rose, "How Did the Smallpox Vaccination Program Come About?" in Andrew Lakoff and Stephen J. Collier (eds), *Biosecurity Interventions: Global Health and Security in Question* (Columbia University Press, 2008).

28 US Congressional Research Service, "The Strategic National Stockpile," updated 2023.

29 Project BioShield also enabled the FDA to authorize the emergency use of unapproved medical products. See chapter 5 on the Emergency Use Authorization procedure.

30 National Academies Press, Workshop Summary: *The Nation's Medical Countermeasure Stockpile: Opportunities to Improve the Efficiency, Effectiveness, and Sustainability of the CDC Strategic National Stockpile* (2016), p. 14.

31 Robert O'Harrow, Jr., Jon Swaine, and Aaron C. Davis, "Before the Pandemic, Top Contractor Received Billions from Government to Help Prepare the Nation for Biowarfare," *Washington Post*, June 17, 2020.

32 For an analysis of European efforts to stockpile Tamiflu in anticipation of an avian influenza pandemic, see Stefan Elbe, Anne Roemer-Mahler, and Christopher Long, "Securing Circulation Pharmaceutically," *Security Dialogue* 45(5) (2014).

33 Each of the push packages contains 50 tons of emergency health supplies – "enough to fill the belly of a widebody plane," as the 2018 *Washington Post* article put it. These packages included preconfigured caches of 130 containers of antibiotics, syringes, and oxygen tubing. Sun, "Inside the Secret US Stockpile."

34 US Congressional Research Service, "The Strategic National Stockpile," updated 2023.

35 Kadlec continued: "Mother Nature doesn't develop highly virulent organisms that are resistant to our current stockpiles of antibiotics." Jon Swaine, Robert O'Harrow, Jr., and Aaron C. Davis, "Before Pandemic, Trump's Stockpile Chief Put Focus on Biodefense," *Washington Post*, May 4, 2020.

36 In 2017, as the *Washington Post* reported in an investigative article, Emergent's corporate strategy aimed to shift the federal management of the stockpile from the CDC to the ASPR. Soon after Kadlec's appointment as Assistant Secretary for Preparedness and Response, this shift was made. Swaine, O'Harrow, Jr., and Davis, "Before Pandemic."

37 Swaine, O'Harrow, Jr., and Davis, "Before Pandemic."

38 Swaine, O'Harrow, Jr., and Davis, "Before Pandemic."

39 Sarah Kliff, "US Hospitals Prepare for Coronavirus, With the Worst Still to Come," *New York Times*, March 12, 2020. In May, the *Washington Post* pointed out that the 2019 Crimson Contagion exercise – coordinated by Kadlec's office – had found that officials would face cascading supply chain shortages, including "scarce medical countermeasures such as personal protective equipment, diagnostics, and antivirals." Swaine, O'Harrow, Jr., and Davis, "Before Pandemic."

40 US Congressional Research Service, "The Strategic National Stockpile," updated 2023.

Chapter 4 The Scenario-Based Exercise

1 The White House, "Members of the Coronavirus Task Force Hold a Press Briefing, March 19, 2020." Accessed at: https://it.usembassy.gov/members-of-the-coronavirus-task-force-hold-a-press-briefing-march-19-2020/

2 David E. Sanger, Eric Lipton, Eileen Sullivan, and Michael Crowley, "Before Virus Outbreak, a Cascade of Warnings Went Unheeded," *New York Times*, March 20, 2020.

3 Amy Maxmen and Jeff Tollefson, "The Problem with Pandemic Planning," *Nature* 584 (August 2020).

4 Nahal Toosi, Daniel Lippman, and Dan Diamond, "Before Trump's Inauguration, A Warning: 'The Worst Pandemic Since 1918,'" *Politico*, March 16, 2020.

5 Lena H. Sun, "Top White House Office in Charge of Pandemic Response Exits Abruptly," *Washington Post*, March 10, 2018. On the establishment of the NSC Directorate of Global Health and Biodefense by the Obama administration after the 2014 Ebola epidemic, see Christopher Kirchhoff, "Ebola Should Have Immunized the United States to the Coronavirus," *Foreign Affairs*, March 28, 2020.

6 Maxmen and Tollefson, "The Problem with Pandemic Planning," p. 26.

7 Susan E. Rice, "The Government has Failed on Coronavirus, but There is Still Time," *New York Times*, March 13, 2020.

8 Kirchhoff, "Ebola Should Have Immunized the United States to the Coronavirus."

9 Niklas Luhmann, *Risk: A Sociological Theory* (Routledge, 2005), p. 16.

10 The challenge of managing such catastrophic risks is a central theme of Ulrich Beck's classic discussion of "risk society." Ulrich Beck, *Risk Society: Towards a New Modernity* (Sage, 1992).

11 For an analysis of scenario-based planning as a technology of uncertainty, see Limor Samimian-Darash, *Uncertainty by Design: Preparing for the Future with Scenario Technology* (Cornell University Press, 2022); Ben Anderson distinguishes among three

forms of governmental anticipation in "Preemption, Precaution, Preparedness: Anticipatory Action and Future Geographies," *Progress in Human Geography* 34(6) (2010); for the distinction between risk management and preparedness, see Andrew Lakoff, "Preparing for the Next Emergency," *Public Culture* 19(2) (2007).

12 For a detailed discussion, see Andrew Lakoff, "The Generic Biothreat, or, How We Became Unprepared," *Cultural Anthropology* 23(3) (2008): 399–428.

13 War mobilization was the initial context for the impetus to develop national preparedness plans, as in the lead-up to US involvement in both World War I and World War II.

14 Office of Defense Mobilization, *Mobilization Plan D-Minus* (1957). For the role of the Office of Defense Mobilization in nuclear preparedness planning during the 1950s, see Collier and Lakoff, *The Government of Emergency*.

15 According to Innis Harris of ODM's Plans and Readiness Office, this "war-gaming undertaking" was initiated in 1954 at the behest of President Eisenhower in order to test ODM's provisional mobilization plan. As Harris writes, "The President's reaction to the plan was this: No plan is any better than it works. Test it. And that is how we got started on test exercises – an activity entirely new to the Federal Government." Innis Harris, "Lessons Learned from Operations Alert 1955–1957," cited in Collier and Lakoff, *The Government of Emergency*, p. 266.

16 The quotation is from mobilization planner Shaw Livermore, cited in *The Government of Emergency*, p. 266.

17 Cabinet Paper, "Operation Alert 1957" (The White House, May 20, 1957). Accessed at: https://www.eisenhowerlibrary.gov/sites/default/files/finding-aids/pdf/who-oss/cabinet-minutes-series.pdf

18 The Operation Alert exercises were held in collaboration with the Federal Civil Defense Agency.

19 Memo from Willard Paul (1954), cited in Collier and Lakoff, *The Government of Emergency*, p. 271.

20 Harris, "Lessons Learned." The 1955 Operation Alert exercise

and its impact on the debate within the executive branch over the "chain of command" in a future wartime emergency is described in more detail in Stephen J. Collier and Andrew Lakoff, The Government of Emergency: Vital Systems, Expertise, and the Politics of Security (Princeton University Press, 2021).

21 Cited in Collier and Lakoff, *The Government of Emergency*, p. 265.

22 Executive Office of the President, Office of Emergency Planning, 1964. *The National Plan for Emergency Preparedness.* Accessed at: https://biotech.law.lsu.edu/climate/FEMA/npep-1964.pdf

23 Scott Knowles, *The Disaster Experts: Mastering Risk in Modern America* (University of Pennsylvania Press, 2013).

24 Andrew Lakoff, *Unprepared: Global Health in a Time of Emergency* (University of California Press, 2017).

25 Homeland Security Council, *National Strategy for Pandemic Influenza* (2005), p. 2.

26 US Department of Health and Human Services, Office of the Assistant Secretary for Preparedness and Response, *Crimson Contagion 2019 Functional Exercise After Action Report* (January 2020), p. 14.

27 HSS did not release the report to the public, but it was made available by the *New York Times* as a link in its article on the exercise that appeared in March 2020. Sanger, Lipton, Sullivan, and Crowley, "Before Virus Outbreak, a Cascade of Warnings Went Unheeded."

28 Certain of the report's recommendations on administrative reform proved to be prescient during the early stages of the federal response to Covid-19. For instance, while HHS was initially designated the lead agency for the federal response, on March 19, 2020, shortly after the president's declaration of a "national emergency" under the Stafford Act, the FEMA assumed the lead for the federal response so that emergency relief funds could be accessed.

Chapter 5 Emergency Use

1 US Department of Defense, "Coronavirus: DOD Response." Accessed at: https://www.defense.gov/Explore/Spotlight/Coronavirus/Operation-Warp-Speed/

2 Theodore M. Porter, *Trust in Numbers: The Pursuit of Objectivity in Science and Public Life* (Princeton University Press, 1995).

3 US Department of Health and Human Services, Administration for Strategic Preparedness and Response, "Project BioShield." Accessed at: https://www.medicalcountermeasures.gov/barda/cbrn/project-bioshield

4 Stuart L. Nightingale, Joanna M. Prasher, and Stewart Simonson, "Emergency Use Authorization (EUA) to Enable Use of Needed Products in Civilian and Military Emergencies," *Emerging Infectious Diseases* 13(7) (2007).

5 US Food and Drug Administration, "Guidance Document: Emergency Use Authorization of Medical Products and Related Authorities" (2017). Accessed at: https://www.fda.gov/regulatory-information/search-fda-guidance-documents/emergency-use-authorization-medical-products-and-related-authorities

6 Stephen J. Collier and Andrew Lakoff, *The Government of Emergency: Vital Systems, Expertise, and the Politics of Security* (Princeton University Press, 2021).

7 Kim Lane Scheppele, "Small Emergencies," *Georgia Law Review* 40 (2005–2006): 837.

8 "Emergency Use Authorization Declaration: A Notice by the Health and Human Services Department on 03/27/2020," *Federal Register: The Daily Journal of the United States Government*, March 27, 2020. Accessed at: https://www.federalregister.gov/documents/2020/03/27/2020-06541/emergency-use-authorization-declaration

9 Eric Topol, "Dear Commissioner Hahn: Tell the Truth or Resign," *Medscape*, August 31, 2020.

10 Sharon LaFraniere, Katie Thomas, Noah Weiland, Peter Baker, and Annie Karni, "Scientists Worry about Political Influence

over Coronavirus Vaccine Project," *New York Times*, August 2, 2020.

11 Katie Thomas, "All Eyes are on Pfizer as Trump Pushes for Vaccine by October." *New York Times*, September 30, 2020.

12 Berkeley Lovelace, Jr. and Noah Higgins-Dunn, "Trump Says US Could Start Distributing a Coronavirus Vaccine in October, Contradicting CDC's Timelines," *CNBC*, September 16, 2020.

13 Topol, "Dear Commissioner Hahn."

14 Patrizia Cavazzoni, Peter Marks, Susan Mayne, et al., "Senior FDA Career Executives: We're Following the Science to Protect Public Health in Pandemic." *USA Today*, September 10, 2020.

15 Jeremy M. Levin, Paul J. Hastings, Ted W. Love, et al. "An Open Letter to the Biopharmaceutical Industry," Biotechnology Innovation Organization, September 3, 2020. Accessed at: https://www.bio.org/sites/default/files/2020-09/An_Open_Letter_to_the_Biopharmaceutical_Industry.pdf. The defense of FDA autonomy by pharmaceutical and biotech industry leaders, who presumably had an interest in accelerating the vaccine authorization process, testifies to the strength of the alliance around the normal regulatory order.

16 Lawrence O. Gostin, "Science, Leadership, and Public Trust in the COVID-19 Pandemic." *The Milbank Quarterly Opinion*, September 28, 2020. Accessed at: https://www.milbank.org/quarterly/opinions/science-leadership-and-public-trust-in-the-covid-19-pandemic/

17 Alec Tyson, Courtney Johnson, and Cary Funk, "US Public Now Divided Over Whether to Get COVID-19 Vaccine," Pew Research Center, September 17, 2020. Accessed at: https://www.pewresearch.org/science/2020/09/17/u-s-public-now-divided-over-whether-to-get-covid-19-vaccine/#:~:text=About%20half%20of%20U.S.%20adults,a%2021%20percentage%20point%20drop.

18 Robert Califf, Scott Gottlieb, Margaret Hamburg, et al., "Opinion: 7 Former FDA Commissioners: The Trump Administration is

Undermining the Credibility of the FDA." *Washington Post*, September 29, 2020.

19 Gil Eyal, *The Crisis of Expertise* (Polity, 2019), pp. 52, 62.

20 Sydney Ember, "Biden, Seizing on Worries of a Rushed Vaccine, Warns Trump Can't Be Trusted," *New York Times*, September 16, 2020.

21 Sam Gringlas, "Public Health Leaders Vow Science, Not Politics, Will Guide COVID-19 Vaccine," *NPR*, September 23, 2020.

22 US Department of Health and Human Services, Food and Drug Administration, Center for Biologics Evaluation and Research, "Emergency Use Authorization for Vaccines to Prevent COVID-19: Guidance for Industry." October 2020. Accessed at: https://www.regulations.gov/document/FDA-2020-D-1137-0019

23 Peter Marks, "The FDA's Vaccines and Related Biological Products Advisory Committee and its Role in Advising the Agency on COVID-19 Vaccines." Accessed at: https://www.fda.gov/news-events/fda-voices/fdas-vaccines-and-related-biological-products-advisory-committee-and-its-role-advising-agency-covid

24 Laurie McGinley, Yasmeen Abutaleb, and Josh Dawsey, "Trump, White House Demand FDA Justify Tough Standards for Coronavirus Vaccine, Raising Concerns of Political Interference." *Washington Post*, September 25, 2020.

25 Sharon LaFraniere and Noah Weiland, "White House Blocks New Coronavirus Vaccine Guidelines," *New York Times*, October 5, 2020.

26 LaFraniere and Weiland, "White House Blocks New Coronavirus Vaccine Guidelines."

27 Califf et al., "Opinion: 7 Former FDA Commissioners."

28 Michelle McMurry-Health, open letter to Alex Azar, Secretary of US Department of Health and Human Services, October 1, 2020. Accessed at: https://www.bio.org/sites/default/files/2020-10/BIO%20Sends%20Letter%20to%20HHS%20Secretary%20Alex%20Azar_0.pdf

29 Antonio Regalado, "One Doctor's Campaign to Stop a Covid-19 Vaccine Being Rushed Through before Election Day," *MIT Technology Review*, October 19, 2020. As the *New York Times* reported: "They slipped a condensed version of the guidelines into the appendix of the committee's briefing materials, with reordered paragraphs and a new title, describing it as a summary of advice already given to companies." Sheila Kaplan, Sharon LaFraniere, Noah Weiland, and Maggie Haberman, "How the FDA Stood Up to the President," *New York Times*, October 20, 2020.

30 Kaplan, LaFraniere, Weiland, and Haberman, "How the FDA Stood Up to the President."

31 Jon Cohen, "Calm Down about Political 'Mischief' Around COVID-19 Vaccines, Scientists Say," *Science*, October 7, 2020. See also David Quammen, *Spillover: Animal Infections and the Next Human Pandemic* (New York: W. W. Norton, 2012).

Chapter 6 Gain of Function

1 David Quammen, "We Made the Coronavirus," *New York Times*, January 28, 2020. See also David Quammen, *Spillover: Animal Infections and the Next Human Pandemic* (New York: W. W. Norton, 2012).

2 Peter Daszak, "We Knew Disease X Was Coming. It's Here Now," *New York Times*, February 27, 2020.

3 Charles Calisher et al., "Statement in Support of the Scientists, Public Health Professionals, and Medical Professionals of China Combatting Covid-19." *The Lancet* 395(10226) (February 19, 2020).

4 Kristian G. Andersen, Andrew Rambaut, W. Ian Lipkin, Edward C. Holmes, and Robert F. Garry, "The Proximal Origin of SARS-CoV-2," *Nature Medicine* 26 (March 17, 2020).

5 World Health Organization, "WHO-convened Global Study of Origins of SARS-CoV-2: China Part." Accessed at: https://www.who.int/docs/default-source/coronaviruse/final-joint-report_origins-studies-6-april-201.pdf

6 World Health Organization, Report by the Director-General.

"Implementation of the International Health Regulations (2005): Report of the Review Committee on the Functioning of the International Health Regulations (2005) in relation to Pandemic (H1N1) 2009." May 5, 2011. Accessed at: https://apps.who.int/gb/ebwha/pdf_files/WHA64/A64_10-en.pdf

7 World Health Organization, Meeting Report: "Report of the Ebola Interim Assessment Panel" (July 1, 2015). Accessed at: https://www.who.int/publications/m/item/report-of-the-ebola-interim-assessment-panel---july-2015

8 World Health Organization, Seventy-Third World Health Assembly, "Covid-19 Response," May 19, 2020. Accessed at: https://apps.who.int/gb/ebwha/pdf_files/WHA73/A73_R1-en.pdf

9 The Independent Panel for Pandemic Preparedness and 8Response, "Covid-19: Make it the Last Pandemic." May 2021. Accessed at: https://theindependentpanel.org/wp-content/uploads/2021/05/COVID-19-Make-it-the-Last-Pandemic_final.pdf

10 World Health Organization, "WHO Director-General's Remarks at the Member State Briefing on the Report of the International Team Studying the Origins of SARS-CoV-2." March 30, 2021. Accessed at: https://www.who.int/director-general/speeches/detail/who-director-general-s-remarks-at-the-member-state-briefing-on-the-report-of-the-international-team-studying-the-origins-of-sars-cov-2

11 Jesse D. Bloom et al., "Investigate the Origins of COVID-19," *Science* 372(6543) (May 14, 2021).

12 Nicholas Wade, "The Origin of COVID: Did People or Nature Open Pandora's Box at Wuhan?" *Bulletin of the Atomic Scientists*, May 5, 2021.

13 McNeil noted in the piece that while there had been an initial consensus on zoonosis among leading virologists, "more and more scientists feel misled." William McNeil, "How I Learned to Stop Worrying and Love the Lab Leak Theory," *Medium*, May 17, 2021. Accessed at: https://donaldgmcneiljr1954.medium.com/how-i-learned-to-stop-worrying-and-love-the-lab-leak-theory-f4f88446b04d

14 Michael R. Gordon, Warren P. Strobel, and Drew Hinshaw, "Intelligence on Sick Staff at Wuhan Lab Fuels Debate on Covid-19 Origin," *Wall Street Journal*, May 23, 2021.
15 Antonio Regalado, "No One Can Find the Animal that Gave People Covid-19," *MIT Technology Review*, March 26, 2021.
16 David Wallace-Wells, "We've Been Talking about the Lab Leak Hypothesis All Wrong," *New York Times*, February 28, 2023.
17 "This is not a contest now, in the public domain, between bodies of evidence," as Quammen put it. "This is a contest between stories." David Quammen, "The Ongoing Mystery of Covid's Origin," *New York Times*, July 25, 2023.
18 An infamous example was the charged congressional hearing, in May 2021, in which Senator Rand Paul accused Anthony Fauci, the director of the National Institute of Allergy and Infectious Diseases, of having violated a moratorium on funding "gain of function" research with his agency's support for coronavirus research at the Wuhan Institute of Virology. Fauci and his fellow science administrators also came under attack for having played a behind-the-scenes role in helping to organize the March 2020 "proximal origin" letter, perhaps to head off concerns about a possible lab accident.
19 The conference led to the publication of an influential 1992 volume under the aegis of the Institute of Medicine. Joshua Lederberg, Robert E. Shope, and Stanley C. Oaks, *Emerging Infections: Microbial Threats to Health in the United States* (National Academies Press, 1992).
20 Stephen S. Morse, "Emerging Viruses: Defining the Rules for Viral Traffic," *Perspectives in Biology and Medicine* 34(3) (Spring 1991).
21 Donald A. Henderson, "Conference on Emerging Viruses: Surveillance Systems and Intergovernmental Cooperation." May 3, 1989. Unpublished manuscript. Accessed at: http://www.zero-pox.info/da_spch/1of6-6_1989_emerge.pdf
22 As anthropologist Lyle Fearnley has shown, the field of

epidemic intelligence, as pioneered by Alexander Langmuir in the 1950s, involved the elaboration of disease surveillance methods for the detection of new epidemics. Lyle Fearnley, "Epidemic Intelligence: Langmuir and the Birth of Disease Surveillance," *Behemoth: A Journal on Civilization* 3(3) (December 2010).

23 Ari Schuler, "Billions for Biodefense: Federal Agency Biodefense Funding, FY2001 – 2005," *Biosecurity and Bioterrorism* 2(2) (2004).

24 David L. Heymann and Guénaël Rodier, "Global Surveillance, National Surveillance, and SARS," *Emerging Infectious Diseases* 10(2) (2004).

25 As described in chapter 1, the revised IHR also included a requirement for WHO member states to develop "core capacities" for detecting and responding to infectious disease outbreaks.

26 Evan Ratliffe, "The Plague Fighters: Stopping the Next Pandemic Before it Begins," *Wired Magazine*, April 24, 2007.

27 Rebecca Buckman, "Google Philanthropy Director to Take on Disease Outbreaks," *Wall Street Journal*, February 27, 2006.

28 Ratliffe, "The Plague Fighters."

29 "Animal-Borne Diseases? EcoHealth Alliance President Cautions TEDMED Conference Attendees to 'Be Afraid . . . Be Very Afraid.'" *PRNewswire*, October 27, 2010. Accessed at: https://www.prnewswire.com/news-releases/animal-borne-diseases-ecohealth-alliance-president-peter-daszak-cautions-tedmed-conference-attendees-to-be-afraidbe-very-afraid-105918313.html

30 Laurie Garrett, "The Next Pandemic?" *Foreign Affairs* 84(4) (July–August 2005). For an ethnographic study of the management of avian influenza in East Asia, see Frédéric Keck, *Avian Reservoirs: Virus Hunters and Birdwatchers in Chinese Sentinel Post* (Duke University Press, 2020).

31 Yi Guan, Richard Webby, Ilaria Capua, and Jonas Waldenstrom, "H5N1: How to Track a Flu Virus." *Nature* 483 (March 28, 2012).

32 For a more detailed examination of the debate over the risks

and benefits of gain-of-function research on the H5N1 virus, see Lakoff, *Unprepared*, ch. 5.

33 US Department of Health and Human Services, *HHS Pandemic Influenza Plan* (November 2005). Accessed at: https://www.cdc.gov/flu/pdf/professionals/hhspandemicinfluenzaplan.pdf

34 National Institute of Allergy and Infectious Disease, *Report of the Blue Ribbon Panel on Influenza Research*, September 11–12, 2006.

35 Deborah Cohen and Philip Carter, "WHO and the Pandemic Flu 'Conspiracies,'" *British Medical Journal* 340 (June 4, 2010).

36 See Peter Palese and Taia T. Wang, "H5N1 Influenza Viruses: Facts, not Fear," *Proceedings of the National Academy of Sciences* 109(7) (January 25, 2012).

37 Denise Grady and Donald G. McNeil, Jr., "Debate Persists on Deadly Flu Made Airborne," *New York Times*, December 26, 2011.

38 Anthony S. Fauci, Gary J. Nabel, and Francis S. Collins, "A Flu Risk Worth Taking," *Washington Post*, December 30, 2011.

39 Declan Butler, "Flu Surveillance Lacking," *Nature* 483 (March 28, 2012).

40 Simon Wain-Hobson, "H5N1 Viral-engineering Dangers Will Not Go Away," *Nature* 495 (March 27, 2013).

41 W. Paul Duprex, Ron A. M. Fouchier, Michael J. Imperiale, Marc Lipsitch, and David A. Relman, "Gain-of-Function Experiments: Time for a Real Debate," *Nature Reviews Microbiology* 13 (December 8, 2014).

42 Jocelyn Kaiser, "Academy Meeting on Risky Virus Studies Struggles to Find Common Ground," *Science*, December 17, 2014.

43 Peter Daszak, "Understanding the Risk of Bat Coronavirus Emergence." Accessed at: https://grantome.com/grant/NIH/R01-AI110964-06

44 Over the course of the pandemic, more details of the experimental program gradually emerged, in many cases due to the research of "internet sleuths" who were able to access documents

such as a grant proposal made to DARPA by EcoHealth Alliance in collaboration with the Wuhan Institute that proposed to insert a novel furin cleavage site into the spike proteins of SARS-related coronaviruses in the laboratory. For a helpful overview, see Carolyn Kormann, "The Mysterious Case of the Covid-19 Lab-Leak Theory," *New Yorker*, October 12, 2021.

Epilogue

1 Senate Committee on Homeland Security and Governmental Affairs, "Full Committee Hearing: Preparedness for Covid-19: The Initial Pandemic Response and Lessons Learned," April 14, 2021. Accessed at: https://www.hsgac.senate.gov/hearings/preparedness-for-covid-19-the-initial-pandemic-response-and-lessons-learned/

Index